LOOKING FOR MAN

Brian Lewis was born in Birmingham in 1936. This teacher, critic, publisher, writer and painter has lived in Pontefract since 1960. He has written over fifty books on a range of topics, including six books of poetry in the Jude series. Recently elected Deputy Chairman of Yorkshire Arts, he was also Birmingham's first Poet Laureate in 1996. Brian is currently Visiting Fellow in Verse and Fine Art at Loughborough University. In 1999 he was awarded an honorary doctorate by Sheffield Hallam University.

LOOKING FOR MANDY'S PLACE

AN EPIC MILLENNIUM POEM

*Who is this Alexander Pope I hear so much about. I cannot
discover what is his merit. Why will my subjects not write in prose?*

George II

*If in this Testament there be
any sort of difficulty
I give you my full authority
to prune it like an apple tree.*

François Villon 1416

Brian Lewis
1999

Loughborough University School of Art & Design, Leicestershire.

Looking for Mandy's Place

Brian Lewis

Illustrations by Colin Rhodes
With essays by Vic Allen and David Godber

Published by Loughborough University School of Art & Design
in association with Pontefract Press

First published 1999

© Brian Lewis, Colin Rhodes and Loughborough University

ISBN 1 900856 40 9

Layout and cover design by Mark Wood

The moral rights of the authors have been asserted.

Loughborough University
School of Art & Design
Loughborough
Leicestershire
LE11 3BT

Pontefract Press
17 Linden Terrace
Pontefract
West Yorkshire
WF8 4AE

Contents

Introduction by Vic Allen 7

Prologue 12

Canto One
In which Jude, a northern girl who is under–employed, traverses a tunnel underneath the Thames looking for a cafe called *Mandy's Place*. She finds the Greenwich Car Boot Sale and listens to orators. 14

Canto Two
In which Jude meets Karen, a girl she once worked with at Tescos. They talk about Karen's travelling man and the romance that you find at car boot sales. Both say that although they are going to find *Mandy's Place* neither has a clear idea of what is meant by the phrase 28

Canto Three
In which Jude and Karen discuss food, Queen Mab and the nature of Wormholes before going down one. 40

Canto Four
In which Ram, Karen, the children and Jude travel on the Docklands Light Railway looking at Winos, feisty girls and wondering about the significance of mobile phones and the status of people who do not use them. 48

Canto Five
In which Jude looks across at the Dome and wonders if this really is Mandy's Place and then locates the cornershop where Ram has an attic flat. 58

Canto Six
In which Jude listens to Zarathustra (an alias) and meets Mills and Boon. They talk about the death of Di and Dodi and explain the plot of *The Nation's Loss* 68

Canto Seven
In which conversations take place about nicknames, coalmining communities, important pit families and Al Fayed's relatives 78

Canto Eight

In which Karen's Ex tells of his love of Loughborough and
the Rise and Fall of the Ladybird Empire. 86

Canto Nine

In which Jude and Karen meet Mandy. They were all at
school together. They walk to the Observatory. After looking
through a telescope Jude decides to go and look at the Dome
from close up. 102

Canto Ten

In which they see the inside of the Dome, meet a poet
and get a lot of explanations, alliances are made, there
are transformations, but not everything ends happily
ever after. 120

Epilogue 142

Essay by David Godber 145

Introduction

A physician named Merrill Moore wrote at least one sonnet a day for most of his adult life, winding up with so many thousands of sonnets that the reader is discouraged even before he begins reading any of them. Dr. Moore wrote nothing but sonnets, a preoccupation that cannot fail to seem excessive.
Francis Stillman in *The Poet's Manual and Rhyming Dictionary* (Thames and Hudson 1966)

The acropetal nature of Western religion means that domes don't feature much in Albion's architecture. When they do crop up, they are usually—for want of Islamic building skills—con tricks. Most of them are spires, bracketing lead umbrellas aloft and hoisting up cupolas for their underskirts. The best known of these, of course, is St. Paul's Cathedral, while significant but less ambitious ones can also be found in Oxford and at Castle Howard in Yorkshire. If you want a genuine, unsupported dome then you could do worse than go to what was the Royal Devonshire Hospital in Buxton, Derbyshire. Victorians forked out brass merely to enter and marvel at it. Last heard of it was falling into disrepair. Think on that thought, as Brian Lewis would say. What Brian Lewis did say (when he first broached the topic) was that the £800m Millennium Dome budget could cut class sizes across the nation well below the numbers promised by New Labour in its electioneering mode. Evidently this was too modest an achievement to mark the Millennium. It was neither something that would cause the nation to swell with pride nor something that would bring the sponsors running over the hills waving their fat cheque–books.

The Millennium Dome is going to be a success. That is guaranteed, because people are indifferent. The paradigm is British Gas, the first great privatisation of the Thatcher years. You might remember it. The advertising agency Young and Rubicam came up with the slogan 'Tell Sid'. It was arguably the weakest phrase in copywriting history; but blared out at great expense on every public billboard and screen it succeeded. The ministerial use of public funds to avoid political embarrassment is part of the modern electoral contract. The Millennium Dome, too, will be clamourously Blaired out; it will become a veritable *tumour* of success. This is precisely why Simon Armitage, the 'neat young man' who appears here in Canto Ten, has been commissioned to write a Dome's day book about 'The Millennium Experience'. He's a good and popular poet, but controversy was never his song; Brian Lewis quite fairly suggests that he 'is paid to see the magic of the place and scribble forth'. *Looking for Mandy's Place* is an antidote to such hype.

The first time I met Brian was to interview him about *The Quest for the Plastic Grail*, the first of his sagas featuring Jude to get into print. It was, like *Mandy's Place*, an epic told in sonnets and I had made a discovery about the book that seemed to me immensely acute.

'Some of these sonnets have got 15 lines!' I trounced him.

'Oh. Have they?' came the mildly intrigued response.

Then, no less obliviously. 'Let's see. Oh yes... so they do. Well.' And that was about it. Brian is not obsessive about form. You will find one line in this book with 18 syllables, and another with 9. Gerard Manley Hopkins invented a unique form of maths to justify such waywardness; Brian hasn't and wouldn't. Neither is Brian concerned about feeling in poetry. He shares nothing with those who 'See verse as deep emotion in disguise.' Form and emotion: the two essential ingredients of art as we know it and Brian can't be arsed with either of them. You might find this a fault... Welcome to the club. I find this a fault. Brian is the kind of man who, if he had two hours to visit the Museum of Modern Art in New York, would be deeply content to spend them talking to an invigilator; discovering their attitude to the art they were zookeepering, what they thought of the punters, and what they were paid. Art without people doesn't make a lot of sense to Brian. You might find this a fault... I don't. Form your own club.

Jude is Brian's 'Everyman' and as befits a true 'Everyperson' in 1999 she doesn't read much poetry. She knows a bit about graduates but isn't one; she knows a bit about tarot, but is not tempted by divination; ditto art, science, and philosophy. Crucially, Jude has no pretensions; she hasn't swallowed the designedly disabling bait that links cultural attainment to self worth. But equally crucially, she is no Orwellian 'prole'. She is emphatically *not* a BBC 'working class person'. She has walked outside the cage of her personality in a way that the cast of 'Eastenders' would never be allowed to do. When Brian refers to: 'common sense, a sense found in the working class', it is reasonably safe to credit him with referencing fellow trade unionist Antonio Gramsci (1891–1937), rather than the dullard's idea of 'common sense' as a collection of rusty saws and fondly pampered bigotry.

The idealised hero of *Mandy's Place* is 'Longitude' Harrison (1692–1776), the John who made the most significant contribution to the shipboard chronometer and thus made navigation in all weathers possible.

'No theorist Harrison; his Maths weren't pure.
      Like Christ he was a carpenter and cut his stops
      and cogs from lignum vitae...'

Harrison is pertinent to Greenwich, of course, and to Jude (St Jude was a carpenter); but also to Gramsci, who came as close as most Bolsheviks will allow to defining an amenable form of intellectual—namely the 'organic intellectual': 'Each man... carries on some form of intellectual activity, that is, he is a "philosopher", an artist, a man of taste', Gramsci argued, distinguishing between a priest, say, and a person like John Harrison. Organic intellectuals such as Jude can be distinguished because, like an organic carrot, they are fed on bullshit. It is the need to process this bullshit, to constantly question information without being driven into a socially exclusive radicalism that leads Brian to his wayward style. The Tory maverick Alan Clark once said—in one of those questionnaires that proved to be the single contribution of the evanescent *Correspondent* to modern journalism—that the thing he 'hated most in the world' was the rhythm of John Skelton. Imagine! 400 years on, and the puerile form (not, note, the content) of Skeltonics still has the power to offend the ruling class. The Barnsley bard Ian McMillan has just written a book of joyously jangling poems devoted to Barnsley Football Club. It was critically dismissed by at least one football magazine as 'terrible poetry'. Dominant in the cultural arena, sports writers today are of course referees of all they survey; but Alan Clark's lingering distaste for Skelton suggests to me that it's a lickspittle critic who dismisses doggerel out of hand.

'In truth she is not really bad,
      just dangerous to know. A poppet almost...'

This is a typical piece of Lewis–speak; a conflation of the archaic ('In truth...'), the historical ('Mad, bad and dangerous to know'—Lady Caroline Lamb speaking of another rambling scribe), and the northern vernacular ('poppet'). This is no *blend*; no hackneyed, establishment–pleasing 'celebration' of the English language. It is both usage and abusage. As Brian notes, ironically, 'Today it's style that counts'. Which makes it essential to avoid style, to avoid decorum, to avoid 'cool'.

Brian's disinterest in form reflects a similar political distrust:

'I hate a world where neat

Ideas form rows and hold the sylvan landscape in the grip
Of order.'

The first of the Jude Sagas, *The Book of Jude*, features a love–struck dumpling who—like her near biblical namesake— slices off her lover's head. It has Brian's droll tone and hypertrophied world–view, but the poised construction is distinctly two dimensional. In the later Jude sagas Brian abandons plot in favour of conjoining, like an amatory frog, with literary myths such as Mallory's *Le Morte d'Arthur*, or Dante's *Divine Comedy*. The parody that results amplifies Brian's humour, but the artificial construction also takes him away from what he knows best. Here, in *Mandy's Place*, Brian has arrived at a model of construction that suits his aims. It's digressive. You'll hardly need persuading of this.

'The plot will never over
boil if we stand by to chew this cud.'

And it ignores time as happily as any other authoritarian form of gubernance.

'In every brain there are two clocks. One is a stop watch, the
other takes the Time Frame of a day. What brings confusion
into reckonings is mixing of two clocks which do not match.'

The point is that time is a commodity which, like any other commodity, can be dealt with on the ideological stock market. As Brian, and many other non–Millenarians have pointed out, to half the world: 'The year is 1378'.

It is interesting that Brian has always been a man for 'Hobby Horses': the Royal Family is an instance. A recent cruise of the bookshelves revealed that my very first encounter with Brian had been an unwitting one. Throwing out a clag of unwanted poetry books from an office that I had moved into, my eye was caught by a red, white and blue volume. It was *The Divorce*— a series of poems devoted to the sorry marriage of Charles Windsor and Diana Spencer. The sheer vulgarity of it was breathtaking. I also liked the slogan on the back—not only for it's political sentiments, but also for its potential as a strapline on the next movie outing for Ridley Scott's Aliens. It read, 'You have no histories. History is theirs'. Brian essentially deals in recent history; he is at the carcass while the hook–beaked journalists are still picking over it, but before the bone–smashing historians lumber in. It's a curious hinterland; full of nostalgia, yet lacking allure—like last night's fish supper. Who, even now, will recall the minor brouhaha caused by the extravagant claim upon the public purse of Lord Irving's wallpaper? What reviewer, skimming the book under pressure of deadlines, will fail to remark how Peter Mandelson long since passed over his involvement with 'Ricky Rogers' popadom' ...that it is no longer 'Mandy's Place' any more than it is 'Hesser's Place'? Who in a year's time will understand the concept referred to here as being 'on–message'? The Millennium Dome will be a success for all official time, but it is to be hoped that a wayward historian will occasionally put his foot on the literary landmine that is *Mandy's Place*.

Vic Allen

Prologue

The dome has a striking coronal design. As a vaguely futurist edifice erected to commemorate a mythological history on the site of an invented (and Imperial) chronology, it is the perfect figure for conservative modernism. And, as with the monarchy, the people are made to pay £758 million for it in the name of national unity.

Mandy Merck, *After Diana* 1998

This is *The Argument.*

There are no pockets in a shroud;
think on that thought.

Young Jude has lived her life
away from power, lived stainless steel beside the crowd
of silly cows and effers, those who have no taste. The knife
that cuts through butter does not cut into her days and slice
them into pats. That's why she's free to wander, sign the contract
on the dotted line yet know her goods will reach true price
long days before the summer's out.
                    Philosophy?
                              Don't plan, simply react,
knowing that you'll never know of ought with accuracy. Chance
is a fine thing and that is why you cannot take it with you.
Chance encounters are the arbiter. The Reception for The Dance
of Death, and for the Wedding one, will clear you out. That's always true.
In *Everyday* we do not choose, In *Everyday* we must not second guess.

Just like a shroud there are no pockets in a brushed silk bridal dress.

The Unity of Time.
                    Two years have passed since Lady Di
and Dodi died a–speeding through a tunnel underneath the Seine.
(They hit the thirteenth pillar, ill luck that was for sure). The Why
of that calamity was talked out long ago. Now only real plain
Janes and spotted Kevs will mourn these two, (*The Nation's Loss*), place
wreaths of myrtle on her iron gate. And though the good
and gracious may tend to meditate, and see a consequence for our race,
most don't. Most simply think clothes. Most also think food.

The Unity Of Theme.
                    A northern girl called Jude has not seen,
but recently has heard, about a special eating house, a caf; she's heard
of *Mandy's Place*, and now would see it. That's why she's been
in London wandering, observing close perambulations of the effing herd.

Unity of Place.
                    Beneath the Thames, some distance down from London fogs
there is a tunnel linking Greenwich Quay onto that urbane sprawl, the Isle of Dogs.

Canto One

The Cutty Sark

A wen—a fleshy or callous excrescene.
Samuel Johnson—Dictionary of the English Language 1755

But what is to be the purpose of the great wen of all. The Monster (London) called the
'the metropolis of Empire.'
William Cobett—Rural Rides 1831

In which Jude, a northern girl who is under–employed, traverses a tunnel
underneath the Thames looking for a cafe called *Mandy's Place.* She finds the
Greenwich Car Boot Sale and listens to orators.

Who is this girl who trails a hound upon a sky blue string?
(The dog's called Amen.)
                              An Airedale girl from Cas
is Jude; a wit–whip girl who doesn't sing
along the *My Way* song. A sensible Northern Lass,
she's strayed to London looking for a job that's hers
for ever–and–a–day.
                    Clever?
                              Yes. The–ready–steady–go
of economic growth intrigues her, therefore she has no fears
for futures. She's independent. No snotty infant is on tow
nor is a simpering fella. No single mother she, and
not a Working Girl, (a lass who stands and signals cars
with one quick nod in Leeds, in Spencer Place). No Band
of Hope girl either; she's clever, is a girl who'll yet go far.
Jude speaks just as she finds. Looks ahead and then,
a whisper: "Is London just a nauseous, throbbing wen?"

She walks to Greenwich through a tunnel underneath
the Thames (The Thames flows softly till her song is done)
thinking this thought, "Is London just a Wen?"
                              Beggaring belief,
this ragkin and her solitary dog walk all alone
from shore to shore. They want to see the sights.

They leave the Isle of Dogs at just gone ten,
descend the iron cast stair. Various whites
and creams present as gloaming, but then
in small tiled tunnels all is constant glare.
She closes one eye, looks upon a curve of light
and makes towards it. She who will win must dare.
It's lighted thus by day and in the collied night.
A solitary sign: *Cyclists must not race for fun.*

This tunnel leads on to where Longitude's begun.

Ram Bhajan stirs his cosmic stew and plays
the tabla on an Oxo box. His personal stove's
a primus and he squats beside it most days
in the tunnel and as he cooks he chants. Ram loves
his patch. Before him's spread a cloth of tarnished gold
and on it trinkets of the mystic east, (it seems a pound
will purchase most). There's ash upon his hat: Old
as the Cumbrian Hills, he sometimes hears a sound
way up beyond the tiles and bricks. It is the sacred River
Thames, Old Father Thames, rolling to the Medway.
And when he hears, Lord Siva looks on him. (Giver,
Receiver and Retainer, the godhead smiles.)
                                          On delay,
Ram's heart beat is controlled, his temporal body can't decay.
He hears the slow waves roll; sensitive, he feels the spray.

Ram's is a hubble-bubble stew, the sort that chufflings sup
before they go to kip in *Top Shop* doorways, retire to sleep
beneath old coats and threadbare blankets. The cup
that cheers is never close at hand. Most nights they weep,
shiver the night along, wonder why tomorrow never
comes and if the Giro reaches here, will it arrive on time. Old
in their misery they still have thoughts about forever—
and—a—day, their gross horizon is not limited. They're cold
and ill so can't define their feelings. Government junketing has
shown them where they stand.

                         A single mother pulls a cork
from a small bottle. Jude walks on past, thinks, "Was
she one of those who must define herself as seeking work?"
The baby cries. "Has she stability and a comforting home?"

"Do groundlings such as these deserve a Pleasure Dome?"

Amen, her dog, is pulling on her lead. Jude pulls her in.
What has she learnt of *Mandy's Place*? Just this:
it's at the place where Longitude began, that win–
and–lose time by the *Cutty Sark*; that kiss–
and–tell time, Greenwich–on–the–Thames. The rest
is vague.
　　　　There is a bowl—or possibly some bowls—
of fruit. For those who get a mite depressed
there's crumbs of comfort and profiteroles.

"Someday I will find *Mandy's Place* and come to taste
that bowl of fruit that is prepared for those
who put their trust in Mandy. I must make haste,
the show will soon begin. My task is now to choose.

Out from a cardboard box a chuffling gives a shout.
Amen, a mans best friend, is pissing on a lay–about.

A gimmer stands, he watches as the rig–ship *Cutty Sark* rides
in its concrete dock.
　　　　　　　"Long, long ago this schooner cut
into the Seas of China sailing for Typhoo. And yet the tides
were turning when they built the clipper boat and put
a painted quean as figure head; springing from the brow,
a lass in a short shift. It's she who'd danced
at Alloway's Kirk for Tam.
　　　　　　　Before her on the pier now
stood not sprites and ghouls but citizens who chanced
along this morning looking out for bargains.
　　　　　　　　　　　She holds the tail
she'd grabbed from Tam o' Shanter's fleeing mare
as it crossed flowing water, crossed the Alloway brig."
　　　　　　　　　　　　　"Fail
to miss symbols and you miss a lot. Take care
to think things through." She focuses on the crowds, looks around.
"Now I've got here I'll place my powerful feet on solid ground."

Jude glanced an aged gimmer as she passed and thought
"A mariner for sure. One who sways at tide time, one
who rides the Doldrums out and grins. I guess he's caught
his breath in many Westerlies, has this small man, he's stood alone
on the top mast and seen the nimbostratus break to
smaller pieces as the sun comes up."

                                  She is mistaken;
he was a clerk, an ancient scribe of sorts, not one who
sat in porches as wedding guests arrived there to awaken
images of death in them, to show that immortality
is always round your neck if there they've hung an albatross.
Now he's a looker–on, one who ponders the immorality
of giving fattest cats more cream. Profit and loss
concerns him, not destiny or an ancient clipper ship.

Was the tail in *Cutty Sark's* small hand a harlot's whip?

It's true he loves the language of all ships and is enthralled
by nautical terms and phrases; he's tipped them to his tongue
so that with practice he can roll them forth. Two have called
to him today; *hard tack* and *weevil biscuit*; words that have sprung
from distant voyaging. Words ancient as old rope, real brass–bound
words spring forth as well: *sheep shank, small bends* and *hitches,*
close cleaves, main braces, mizzen mast, sail (for rope); sea sound
words which hang upon your ear; a shoal of nautical riches.

Imagination is his deck, yet here he listens for the bell
that summons forth a Scottish Witch. She could excite,
for though a carv–ed figure–head, the blooming swell
of the well formed breasts — these sepulchre white —
quite turn him on.
                      But then old gimmers know death
is a cantering, spectral horse with tainted breath.

The pierhead is a car boot sale times ten. Here West
met East across meridians; and, via a walking tunnel, South
meets North. Paste table stalls everywhere, those who get the best
come early doors and walk the aisles with a closed mouth.
They use a scanning eye, and speak their wants as if they had
authority. Collectors do not pause to say, "How much is that?"
but state a sure, keen price. A piece that's good or bad
gets treated thus by folks who know what they are at.

What do they seek?
                              Now there's a problem for a May–
morn–walking maid. Emerging from the Tunnel and
seeing such a crowd she speaks her piece. "Who can say
just what we seek when we trail quays to scan
small stalls made up from folding tables ?"

                              Upon his little drum
Ram rat–tat–tats on Golden Kingdoms yet to come.

This is the Millennium Sale. Apocalypse expected, all bring
small gear to place on folding pasting tables.
                              The wedding mug
by Churchill, England; (*Charles with Di–Ich Dien*). A ring
Granny left to a best friend. A clothes horse, (a peggy rug
whose centre has a scarlet spot cut from a Life Guard's
best) straggling it. Next, women's lacy knickers. (A man
in a soft hat looks on these with longing in his eyes.) Shards
from a broken pot glued into place with love, beside a can
of black–eyed *Bachelor's Beans* which looks pre–war, for rust
has brushed its bottom. It stands upon an Art Deco commode.
Sunday school gifts and biblical mottos; *In God We Trust*,
scrolled beneath a soldier with a glazed eye. Spode
plates, Fabergé eggs, foolscap envelopes; objects of desire,
mixed in with junk and remnants from some warehouse fire.

Most houses have a space where bobs and bits like these
get stowed; they haunt the pantry's furthest point in cardboard
boxes, so are like the *Word Hoard*. A natural wish to please
yourself ensures their presence, they are the whip cord
in our world, are there to hold tarpaulins in their place
and guarantee we're dry. What is it hucksters say:
"Hold on to water proofs". Dirty canvas has no grace
yet, don't sell a rain proof even on a sunny day.

The pier is very crowded. A woman with a leather bag
around her neck goes round about taking up the small coin.
She is *The Council*. Everybody knows her, so does not blag
her oft or tight across her eyes draw wool. (Find
treasures such as she, then hold them to you fast,
these car–boot people know that one for sure.)

Elastoplast

has always held the world in place, not grand designs.
Most want a coffee in a coffee shop not *Mandy's Place*
or *Dodi's* splendid *Tomb*. Look round about; card tricks and signs
are everywhere to see. Those who do not hold the Ace
will still buy trifles; glass animals, pot pourri, a dainty silken shoe,
not tickets to the *Ballets Royal*. The reference points are *I Spy
Books* and *Ladybirds*. They think the royals a motley crew
and rarely mell along the Mall. Their wallpaper is forever DIY.

(Its not the sort the Chancellor Irvine puts upon
his wall to fright the tasteless so they cry in guilt,
"By gum," and feel unsure. But then, yon Irvine is a con,
a lawyer in a full blown wig, his wife's a con as well. Up to the hilt
in grandeur, his *obiter dicta*, is never, as it should be, compromise.
It's woolsack wool that's pulled across our eyes.)

With straightened back Jude just strolls on. She's reached a row
of men who stand on stools and roar. Solitaires all,
they talk about the Greenwich Gods.
                                    One says, "All's show,
it's in the mind we live."
                            There is another. His call
is to a God of Malice, one of little mercy. His cry goes thus:
"*The End is Nigh*. I have the gift of tongues. Repent, Repent.
I am elect of God, a sheep and not a goat."
                                    "*Them and uz*
speech that," thinks Jude. Another says that money spent
on tombs and domes should go to feed the poor.
This sullen stands unruffled. She thinks, If I had choice —
and few folk do — I'd listen longer to this speech; sure
footed is this dude. This one's not a man of ice,
I'd take him to my truckle bed and snuggle up; fire
is in his eyes. With one like him to snuggle to, I'd never tire.

Al "Cool" Britannia is this smart dude's name, at least
the name he goes by in the Inns (and Outs) of Court.
(A lawyer he; called Alan by his Mam). The beast
with two backs raunching in a ginnel, fraught
and frazzled, cannnot match this legal mankin's
style. A wencher with an intellect, each easy ride
he ticks off in a different filo fax. All in all his sins
are four: lust, gluttony, avarice and rampant pride.

This man of law, who preached upon the quay most
Sabbath days and sometimes of an evening, awoke
in her the hots and blocked her throat which was toast
warm. He took deep breaths so when he spoke
his words conveyed both passion and security.
                                    Socialist or
Socialite? Neither. A soapy orator, rotten to his very core.

His words were rhetoric, bombast, bluster, blast;
and though *the poor* and *underclass*, his constant themes,
few were convinced. He hammered hard upon an iron last
when most bought shoes from *Clark's*. The dream
of Old John Ball—all men are equal—when he ranted
was never to the fore, for Vladimir Illych is his man,
and so he speaks of infantile disorders. Tainted
is his breath. He focuses upon a Seven Year Plan
that Soviets complete just short of five.

                                        He mentions oft the poor,
Upon the Dome, he has some doubts but says that builders' jobs
will come to the Greenwich Town, that much for sure.
When once they've dropped in foundation stones and bobs,
and architectural bits, are there laid out, all will be
well. Full employment, he reveals, is the real key.

Last one, a chuffling in a rugby shirt, a patchwork Harlequin
each colour drains into another. His theme is also *Dodi's Tomb*
and why the world will come and gawp. Though anorexic thin,
this youth has style and speaks with passion. He says the Dome
is by the *Architect of Tents* Gadafi used, therefore symbolic,
a configuration which holds mysteries. Its ratio is three
times four (Trinity to twelve disciples)—Masonic ,
almost yet also Tantric, at least up to the third degree.

Jude loves the subtlety of ravings such as these;
religion jostles maths, and algebra can calculate
the Laws of Averages yet lacks the as–you–please
of logic and of sense. You have no time to speculate,
the speaker takes short breaths, then whisks you
into realms of gold; where all seems good and true.

One woman and her dog, coasting about looking for
trifles, is that what Jude's about? No, she's much more
than that, she's into real big themes. Some southerners deplore
the bluntness that is found round Leeds, within the core
of towns where she was reared: Glasshoughton, Cas
Fev, most spoke like her, enunciating Ridings twang, (The Aire
and not the Thames, her watering way).
                                        A north country lass
who to London has strayed is Jude so does not care
for etiquette or waving at a limousine. She sleeps on pavements
if she's broke but will not lay her down to lie and wait to see
the corpses of a Queen or Princess trailing by. These ornaments
of royalty—Life Guards carrying the dead and cold; the panoply
of power in one small box silencing a mob—has no appeal but then
she wants equality, to end injustice, wants her fair share.
                                                    Amen.

(Amen's the puppy dog Jude trails on a blue string; it also
is the word that Christian Socialists use to say
debate is at an end and all is well. When Day–Glo
is present as icons and halos and urban decay
has reached its bitter end and all's mint fresh,
that's when they shut their eyes and say "Amen."

For that's your lot and you'd best know it. That crêche,
the future, now seems like the past. A playing pen
which once was pink and cute, a place where heavens above
all once was friendly, now it's just a gaol,
a Bedlam where the things you'd come to love
lie broken and beshitten. New Labour; the nail
you hit upon the head, in several blows lies bent,
the fruits of May, do not seem heaven sent.)

Just why she'd travelled down to Greenwich Pier is not quite
clear. Most northern folk will Whittington way down south
looking for fame. Not her. She's other motives. Delight
in all things which have good report she loves. Into the mouth
of gift horses she does not look. The dark night
of the soul does not descend on her, and why should it,
she's young and agile, lithe and fresh, not up–tight
but neither liberal, rather one whose sense of fun and wit
is gentle. She will never use the oaths that some will
use to make a vulgar point, yet she's direct, though funny
in the prescence of her friends.
                              "Faults?"
                                        "Must I spill
the beans?"
          "Yes."
                "Okay then, lets say an Easter bunny
hides one gift beneath a stone close to a hawthorne break."
"I see, shes less than perfect."
                              "We all make one mistake."

She's travelled down to Greenwich looking for a Grail of sorts
yet what the Grail's about she is not sure. There's
nothing wrong in that, each needs a focus. Any supports
for personality on the move are welcome, shares
in the future come if you've a Grail you wish to hold,
"To have and hold from this day forth as long
as you shall live."
                  Amen.
                        At weddings you are told,
"Don't overstep the mark, patience is a virtue. The song
a girl should sing's a sad song."
                              She'd heard all
that, then when she could not take it any more she up
and left the church. Walked out on family, just walked tall
and moved away.
              (Amen, amen).
                          Her search is for a loving cup
a young girl's Grail. There's symbols everywhere to see
if you look carefully. They're carried three nights weekly on the BBC.

She'd watched the caption of *East Enders*, seen the hard—on
swivel on itself and gently shaft the northern shore.

"Just look at that," her gran had said and pointed. "Upon
the end of that they're building some great *Dome*. Deplore
presumption if you must but you won't stop it".
With that she turned away.
                              Jude looked. Trust
Gran, she's right. It is a prick, you see, if you have wit
enough to start imagining. She's sound — the thrust
is at the north. Although it is a site of dereliction now
its time will come."
                    (*Charles and Diana*, tunnel
vision, sex—drugs and rock—n—roll, concepts to blow
your mind: power, fame and ecstasy, all funnel
to give a hollow echo to the startled primal shout
heard in an underpass.
                      Is that what Dodi's tomb's about?)

The bustle she had met when she emerged has been
replaced just prior to twelve. (The time and place
for bargaining sales is past.)
                              In every market that she'd seen
there is this silent signal. A trader staring into space
sees something odd. Distracted thus he takes a dish,
(often Creamware, Castleford) and wraps it in the *Sun*,
then stows it in a cardboard box.
                                "Is that," she thinks, "a wish
for pastures new or his own kitchen"?
                                    It's noon. Repacking has begun.

To pack a transit van with cardboard boxes is still a real joy.
You've done your duty, made a bob or two so can retire
back to a bolt hole or can wander off. The choice: fry
sausages upon an old domestic Aga or make a brushwood fire
on Otley Chevin and there bake beans. The simple joys
are best. Innocence asks for neither wheres or whys.

Back to the Quay.
              Jude stands alone thinking of this
and that when into focus comes a woman with a
child; in fact, with two. One trails.
                        It's clearly kiss–
and–tell–time, life's High Noon, the moment when decay
seems far away; and so it is. The moment when
upon the Brig yon *Cutty* reaches for the tail of Meg
is twelve hours on. Jude feels depressed. Just then
a mother approaches, speaks direct to her. "I beg
your pardon.
              We've heard of Mandy through TV
and want to find *Her Place*. My tether's at its bitter end.
I've followed every sign there is to get to here. You see
I'm right fed up, foot sore not fancy free. I won't pretend
I can afford it. We live on Family Credit. We are quite lost.
I've travelled on a wayward train so dare not count the cost."

Canto Two

The Journey South

Some are influenced by the love of wealth while others are blindly led on by the mad fever for power and domination but the finest type of woman gives herself up to discovering the purpose and meaning of life itself. She seeks to uncover the secrets of nature. This woman I call a philosopher for although no woman is completely wise in all aspects, she can love wisdom as the key to life's secrets.
Pythagoras of Samos (a little modified)

In which Jude meets a girl she once worked with at Tescos. They talk about Karen's travelling man and the romance that you find at car boot sales. Both say that although they are going to find *Mandy's Place* neither has a clear idea of what is meant by the phrase.

"Don't I know you?"
Of course she does. They worked at Tesco's when
they first left school, they shared a till, but here upon the Greenwich Quay
some doubt has drifted in, she looks quite different but then
who doesn't when you meet them far from home?
To be
recognised away from context requires us to quick make
adjustments in our brain, for usually folk are seen
against a backcloth. Context matters.
(Example: Take
the Wedding Night, love's high flight. Him, ever green,
and she quite innocent of men, moving to a tender kiss
upon the Bucking Balcony. It's summer and the Mall
is all alive with stars, and with dense crowds.
Replace this
moment to a lane near to High Grove. Two weeny people all
alone in brogues and jeans, they're much alive with hope,
pausing for a peck, an erotic whisper; there a joyful grope.

You would not recognise them without a context and
really, why should you? Royals will troop best when on parade,
not close to Stroud; and kissing's not their bag. They stand
aloof from us for they're *Royal Family*. (Can anyone persuade
us otherwise?)

Jude knew this girl. Yes, they had shared a till when
they were fresh sixteen but here upon the Greenwich Quay
she saw she'd lost her fizz and all her sparkle; but then
women age fast in the Northern towns. Believe you me,
the high–tar ciggy smoke will kipper all to bloaters as they
dance up at the Labour Club on Ladies' Night. There time and place
is a constraint. Such girls have little chance. The decay
that is the best is there; it's written on each face
that waltzes past: youth gone, they've lost the need to care.

Jude: "You're Karen Something; lived upon the Square".

Your mother was a Micklethwaite, your aunt sold things
through clubs, collected our small dues on Thursday
nights; she also ran the pools. A brother sings
in Social Clubs the *My Way* song. They pay
their way and though they're unemployed, or on
small score, they never scrounge. The sort who'll
borrow sugar in a china cup and then return it. Won
raffle prizes will get shared around. No one is cool,
no one laid back, for yours is family life lived
like a bowl of fruit. You lie together till you rot.
Yet you observe the rules. You've always sieved
your flour.
      You know what's good from what is not;
the backbone of the English nation, you have no fear.

How did you reach this Quay? Why are you here?"

She gave a sniff, adjusted, then told Jude about her day.

"I rose that minute when my Argos clock gave
off a cockerel call (a–doodle–do). I don't delay
on mornings when the sun is high. No slave
to golden slumbers me. I rather am the sort of miss
who rises up and with the dawn prepares her bloke
a step of dripping bread. The type who gives a kiss
then waves him off at five. Once when I have awoke
I am the sort of lass who'll never trespass back
to swan in bed and snuggle down upon his imprint,
nor will I waste the day till noon with *Marie Claire*. No slack
lass me but one who'll polish up the mantle pieces, do a stint
at Nestlé—four pm to eight—go to a social at the Labour Club
for sing–along and then to bed for gentle rub–a–dub.

I am the marrying sort, though truth to tell
these days I don't know man.
                          My time had come when,
on heat, back to a baker's wall, I quick caught on. Well,
before the Orgreave rout was my first time. Then,
picketing over, he took to travelling and so had
wandered off, and in a hard man's hat, had driven headings.
Some Saturdays back, these not too often. Yet never bad,
just feckless (or so his tattoos said). Readings
of his Tarot showed me the Wandering Man
or else the hanging one, the man who looked
ahead, one leg crossed upon other. Dead pan
my David's face and in that pan his goose was cooked."

Jude looked her up and down then thought, "I know her well enough.
At school she was the Micklethwaite who didn't give a chuff."

Now Karen speaks in a shy whisper,
                          "Discomforted, neglected
yet I still heard the wind as it moved through wastes of fern. Rain
was my comforting neighbour.
                          Innocently happy until selected
early, well before eleven plus, I felt some academic strain.
That's when I looked up to the panoply of stars and thought
about the universe in wonder. Dazzled, but not a well spent
force, no white dwarf me. I had a future well before I caught
my hair in life's entanglements." In scarce a whisper she went
on. "Astronomy; in that I passed *Starred A*, but eleven GCEs
also sat upon my print—out. In every way the form's fast cat.
I was destined for great things but then to please
a Catholic parent I offed to work the Tesco's tills."
                          "VAT
is on most things, with Peter's pennies all are taxed,
but never value added," so said Jude.
                          "How can I be relaxed

with such a history? Then in a floral frock I served
some time in a neat restaurant, at *Little Chef*, the one that stood
at Crecy's Corner, Featherstone. That job unnerved
me; all was so legit. The government stoppages would
have made St Francis destitute. I quit. Next fixing
mobile phones for men whose underclothes were Calvin Klein's,
with ties by Gucci, that became my trade. When mixing
with this class I heard the echoing of taste. Choice wines
as Christmas perks were mine.
                              Spoiling gives girls pressure points
so they respond, not me, I knew my place and though
I went to parties with nibbles in a bowl, when the joints
were rolled I looked away. When men threw up I did not show
disgust but went into the kitchen, found the Dettol, took the mop
and scrubbed. The second baby came and caught me on the hop."

Jude knew her story from way back. Her second daughter Kay
was born in Fryston–on–the–Aire.
                              Jude: 'Didn't he come back
and, slack cat you, you let him lie three nights, beneath your duvet.'

"No, only once – I had the hots. Then blue back–pack
loose held upon his shoulder next day with simple, "See yer',
he went wandering off down to the town of Pontefract
to get his Giro.
                Caught on again, one year
quick concertinaed into five before I got my act
together, said, 'Sad rat–bag, he won't be the last
of my great lovers,' (though actually he was). Once my man
but isn't that no more. I'm now a woman with a past
and two small kids. Henceforth the game of catch–catch–can
I will not play with such as he. Corrupt and stale
this creep. He farts when he breathes out."
                              Jude knew that sort of tale.

Jude knew that type of girlie tale, had heard some part when last
they'd met. Jude tried to think where that place was but could
not say. It might have been in Rotherham or Leeds. The past
will always be another town.

Jude speaks directly:

"Would
you know of Mandy's Place?"

"Of course tomorrow and
the following day we're going there," said Karen, "I work
an extra shift a week to get to visit. I've heard it's grand."
"Better than Betty's," Jude said. (Betty's is a restaurant in York
and that's the best there is.) I've heard that it's a wonder dome
which has a fridgidaire that is frost free. It's *Toys–Я–Us*
with food but on a massive scale. There trolleys roll and come
to rest with wheels aligned. Gadgets everywhere. Without much fuss,
and hardly any queues, a man can gad around that eating space
sampling."

Simpleton. Who knows what will go off in Mandy's Place?

Karen: "This is no season of gob smackery, it is a dull,
dull age. Elegance of language and romance lies
sleeping in shop doorways as we speak. Believe you me the pull
and yank of both are slack, especially in the North. Surprise,
adventure both are dead. The unthinking say, 'We've seen it all
before and know we will again,' but I'm less sure. If there's a plot
I cannot sus it. That's why I've turned to Science. That pall
is not yet carried by the undertaking men. And if it is, so what?"

Jude: "Well I'll be blessed. I really thought I knew what you
were at. I saw you as a dumpling, pretty enough but slack;
no imagination, a counter–out of till receipts. Each new
idea a manager had you cherished. You seemed to lack
cohesion, just a wage slave with a poor opinion; just
someone I liked well enough but did not totally trust."

To see her stood close by the *Cutty Sark* was a surprise.
Yet Jude did not know just why she felt that way.
A millennium sale is where you find most sorts.
                                        "It's nice to rise
early and pass the time of day". said Karen now, "I will not stay
in bed for a Sacred Singalong or till *The Archers* ends.
Do that and you'll not know the thrill of bargains, know where—
burglars for sure—sell fraudulent designer gear. A sale sends
spangles down my spine and makes me want to stay there.

I've found some real pearls: *The Ladybird Book of Lady Di,*
the one that stops well short of death; this in a first edition.
Fred Hoyle upon a static universe: *Jagger On Speed, The Why
And Where Of Sensual Massage* and *How To State A Proposition*".

In life a cautious mother of two, she'll take her sporting chance.
Most nights she snuggles in and reads a Mills and Boon romance.

There in a box beneath a pasting table Jude found a treasure
that she'd long looked for.
                                        "It's Shera, He—Man's special friend
the girl who wields the sparring stick and takes pleasure
riding in a battle car with Puma, it's nestled here. Also a book to send
a tingle to my spine. The *Charles and Diana's Wedding* as a pop —
up book (Pull on a tab and he will gently bend and kiss
her full upon the lips.) A marvel made in cardboard, made to stop
the Clock of Being." She buys it in new money.
                                        "This
is a wonder book for sure, and yet it's often found by those
who rummage through the flotsam of The—Age—of—Throw—Away
—And—Bargain—Buy. Nestling on a tray of pantie hose
it is the missing link.
                        Know this.
                                        All moves to decay
in constant ratios, yet these also let us come alive
to possibility. "If I handle this book gently I might survive."

Jude now to Karen "A car boot sale is made for impulse buying.
Once I bought an Indian silver Anna on an excursion
into Wetherby and stowed it close upon my heart; supplying
some deep need.
                    My taste is catholic yet books upon perversion
I will not buy nor will I purchase smalls. In Barnsley you can buy
used scanties from a knicker box if you are poor or so inclined.
I don't but some folks do. Why do they buy? Don't even try
to answer such a question. It's well beyond you. A mind
which will sort through a mix–pick box of bras and pants,
and find some satisfaction there, has some primeval need,
that goes beyond my mind."
                    Jude is a puritan, her wants
are simple, that's why she says, "If things could be, as I read
that things can be in Mills and Boon then I would run
and kiss folk on this quay."
                    Karen: "They're not. Yet jumble's fun

for at some sales you'll also find strong, sombre gear. Wire
hangers carry frocks, the sort you also buy from down–
town charity shops in Castleford. Objects of Desire
a year ago, today they're simply dish–cloth hopeless.
                    The gown
Diana wore when she went forth to grace the ball in Stroud.
This as a replica; the blue one that lacked a lacy strap
to hold the corsage in its place. Today that dress is like the shroud
an undertaker carries in his box of tricks, the wrap—
around he puts upon the corpse when he collects."

(Think well on this. There are no pockets in a wedding dress
nor are there pockets in a shroud. Come, who today respects
a dress code better than the nodding man who combats stress
by simply undertaking? We all make pledges for we wish to show
that we know we are moving towards Death.)
                    Jude makes a silent vow.

She takes her Anna and hurls it from the Greenwich shore
The Thames accepts the gift. The water's choppy, fresh the air.
She looks for no especial miracle here, no jewelled door
to open to reveal just down below the waves a spiral stair
leading to the *Land Of Nod* or else to Hull or on to Hell.

Upon the plain of water that receives her silver gift
there's no disturbance. "London reserve," she thinks.
                                        A slight swell
sends a wave a–lapping at the pier. She stands stock still. The lift
and swell can be deceptive.
                            "Phases of the moon
and gravitas control us two," says Karen, "so you think on."

Down stream a building site beside a gas works. "Soon
that will be significant to all mankind. We've won
Redemption, for here's a spot of dignity and grace.'
Jude looks deep into that landscape.
                            "Take me on to *Mandy's Place.*"

"Take me to *Mandy's Place*." An odd instruction when you think
it through, for just like her she is a visitor to Greenwich town,
and just like her, she has few roots. "Your sink
was full of pots and grease, like mine," says Jude, "If down–
the–plug–hole–time is here today then it's best we stick
together. To wander on to *Mandy's Place* alone creates
a range of problems. Between us we've quick
wit and, in my case, I've dedication."
                            And here she states
the obvious. "Take me to *Mandy's Place*." That is her way for
like the Yorkshire girl she is she knows the way to act;
best be direct, be almost brussen, for at the core
of life is action; therefore she acts upon a fact;
that fact is that she's fit and being fit she will survive.

"We two have ragger–jagger wit," said Jude, "how do you thrive?"

[36]

"I navigate the stars on cloudless nights therefore I have
some latitude," says Karen. "Longitude's a different matter,
it's more complex but has its virtues. Neither am I a slave
or cynic. Some scientists grow that way or else they're hatter—
mad and cannot cope. Tell me all you know about yon
Mandy and her Place. It's everywhere, it's had some real hype."

"I really like this Karen. She knows what is going on.
Take her all in all," says Jude, "she really is my type."

"Let's start. I need some info, data for my data bank."

Jude: "I'll tell you what I know and of my sources."
                                              She paused
for thought. Unusual this. Then with a, "Thank
you dear for asking," said exactly what she knew.
                                    (Nurture caused
Jude to act this way, to be polite, spill all there was upon the cards
in vigorous language.) She spoke with dignity and with due regards.

Of course some of her thoughts are purest fantasy, for all
of us build bouncy castles in the air. When asked about our musing.
the adjective invades. So she replies, "*Mandy's* is some Hall
of Fame and Fortune, a *fabulous* restaurant. Using
her personality and skill she's built a *wondrous* eating place
that sits astride the Thames, it's on the Greenwich ledge;
back of the gasworks. From all that I've heard it's *really ace*,
wonderful, with such decor and fabulous gilt it's on the edge
of understanding. *Post—modern, ironic,* to an A1 degree,
is both its building and gear is all spaced out within.
The chairs are Rennie Macintosh Long—Tom's, plus filigree
of copperwire, Japanic lacquer, Elasticated covers and a pearl pin.

(These adjectival phrases, like creatures in a Shakespearean play,
will strut and bellow, also fret, but will not brook delay.)

"The central hall's bigger than Butlins but cut to twelfths, each wedge is like a piece of cheesy pizza, around the edge a cavity for Brie, cut into this and cheese will stretch beyond your reach. You need a pinch of sage, and as your ballast, *Force Of Gravity*.

Yet girls like us, if we're polite in *Mandy's Place* are very welcome; that's if our dress code's neat and our companion wears a tie from *Ties–Я–Us*. Remember this, all second generation slum dwellers, even folk who live in council maisonettes and buy from corner shops, know this. Because they have etiquette there is small discomfort. A Duchess and those who slave in shoe shops, know the rules. If they're well read and yet know courtesy, courtesy will strength them. This is a class enclave. Equilibria balance the weak and destitute. Least ways I think they do."

 "Enough on Style," says Karen. "Lets move to food and drink."

Canto Three

Queen Mab

Oh then, I see, Queen Mab hath been with you.
She is the fairies' midwife, and she comes
In shape no bigger than an agate stone
On the fore finger of an alderman,
Drawen by a little team of atomies...

William Shakespeare *Romeo & Juliet*

In which Jude and Karen discuss food, Queen Mab and the nature of
Wormholes before going down one.

Jude: "There is a choice of courses, for east meets west
at *Mandy's Place*. The menu: The cheapest meals are white
potatoes, cod boiled in milk with parsley sauce. Best
silver service sets this off a treat. The effect's quite
startling if the linen's Wicklow White and Waterford the glass
which holds the clouded Pernod. Those who're sharp and bright,
and eat at *Mandy's Place*, agree the whiteness is within a class
that's all its own. That's why this meal is almost totally white.

Second choice: ivory and taupe. That meal: *Batchelor's Cream
of Mushroom* slopped upon a parsnip base then etched about
with mustard trails and curd. Light brown rice fills out this scheme.
It's called *Millennium Delicate*; resembles plasterer's grout.

(The last thought is a thought too far, so is ironic and confused.)

Faint in that knowledge Jude sat upon the river bank and mused.

Karen now. "The table waters from the craters on the moon.
(Or so they say; yet how can that fact be I cannot tell.)
Yet I'll believe in all on Mandy's say so. Only a buffoon
would do otherwise. Mandy is always in the know, well
to the fore in everything. How can you doubt?"

                                        "Okay, so
the Moonshine is a long way off but missions aren't impossible
and that's for sure. Have faith. Mandy will do anything to show
she's in control. How did she get the crater water? It's feasible
that some alien voyager came up trumps and in a deal has made
it plain that he'll deliver lunar water that is clap–cold, least ways
until supplies exhaust. That won't be this decade.
Let's look up to her and sing clear *Songs of Praise*
ensuring that her purity lives free of instant fear.

The table water when it comes is waiter borne and crystal clear."

"Yet there are some who lack my confidence, they think
the water has a humbler source, say if it's pure then it is purest
tap; the sort that sits beneath the bubbles in the sink,
or swirls below the blues in lavy bowls. The demurest
do not choose to think about this water source or
of the bladders it's been through."
                                    Karen : 'Soon
it will pass through mine. It's oft been there before."

Jude: 'Best think it's water from the dark side of the moon.'

"That's normal. When we can't confront what's on the cards
we seek to hide our fear, retreat into ourselves to phantasise,
spiral the past to make it into futures. Who guards
the gates of our imagination, who trumps to our surprise,
who makes the welkin ring, who sharpens the keen
knife? Mandy. She's has real power. Is not a might have been."

Karen: "What will Mandy Girl be like? Like a girl on a circus horse
holding the reins as the spotlight touches her golden hair
and she circles bobbing forever?"
                        "Maybe."
                                    "Of course
eventually she'll settle down, to run a restaurant and her profit share
depending on contentment, having the ability to surprise
she will grow rich. She's full of bright ideas
but can you ride on dreams forever?"

                                When thoughts like these arise
Jude goes to overdrive. Mandy thrills her. A few years
on from now she would be just like her, bland with an invoice
book and letter–headed paper; *Jude Unlimited plc*. Ready to cull
and dead–head, less heroic companies by analysing their choice
and rolling over them, embracing consultancies, recognising the pull
of commercial services, she'll draw up tables headed SWOT,
dividing those that have, from those who really just have not.

And what of Mandy? Will she admire a girl like Jude?
Too right she will. For she'll identify with her sort, another
Amazon, one of a regiment of women on the make. No prude
and yet not slack. Like Mandy she is upon a sliding scale. "If I bother
with life's essentials" Jude thinks, "most days I'll not go far.
Today it's style that counts. There's substance in what's next to nowt.
Observe: the chic cats on the catwalk buy a reflective Volvo car
to speed along as if in adverts. The cat–walk girls will never shout,
'I'll see you luv', outside a Ponte pub on Friday night at closing time,
wear micro–skirts, blouses without sleeves, go knickerless, rather
they will wrap up against the cold, be disciplined. Knowing the sublime
is never the ridiculous, they concentrate their minds, and in that state, gather
up thoughts until they are the menu on their very personal lap top
Each has a range of choices. Their's is a Mind within a Body Shop.

With such a mind I have the right to travel and also to track
on backwards. I cannot be constrained by time or place.
Life breaks through literary structures. If literature is a rack
then I'll grow taller by the minute as I think on. You see the ace
I hold is curiosity. Curiosity rules okay. That and imagination.
The universe can be a grain of sand or else a jumbo jet if I so
wish it. 'Oh brave new world.' Ponder on this. Is there a correlation
between ambition and the massing of commodities? All's on show
at *Mandy's Place.*
                    Think thoughts like these and you can find
yourself fast going places. Track forward and as you quickly think,
don't give much time for silent thought. Leave that to Quakers. Behind
each thin man there is fat one. What's on message? Travel backwards, wink
one eye and start again. Never give up. Are there better things to do?
Definitely not. Into a world of dreams Queen Mab will go with you.

And who is Mab? Is she the woman I have often dreamt about,
the harlot with the whip or else a woman making buns
in the kitchen, stirring rumtopf? The one I never doubt
is in control. She who rouses all with the injunction, "Fun's
a fine thing but not a patch on punishment." She
who brings confusion, sorts me out so I lose confidence.
She who throws a six then makes quite sure that I will throw a three.
Mab is eternity, black and hopeless death, the consequence.
I must perform at every childrens' party—*My Consequence*—the one
I can't accomplish because I'd scream; the black mare
upon the midnight bridge, pursued then reaching out. Alone
I just can't make it. Mab's everywhere. I'm watched by Mab. I stare
through space and, looking back, I see that harlot give a toothy smile.
The sprint is my capacity; Mab makes me run the Mile.

Is Mandy Mab, the mobbled queen from nightmare
land, the one who takes a colander to our dreams
and drains them to the dregs? When glazéd eyed we stare
at what there might have been, she just reminds us, schemes
can never turn to visions. Mandy's mistress
of all that she surveys. The lass who cannot share
with playmates. She who has never known distress
whose periods are on time because she wills them there.

Is Mandy Mab the one who came and quickly saw
and always conquered, Godmother in the Ladybird
that Auntie Edna read to us at Horlicks time before
the sandman came to dust our eyes? Mab is absurd
yet always tinsel–fresh. A solitaire, both delicate lad
and lonely lass conjoin in her.
Come, Mandy's mad!

Yes, she is mad, for Queen Mab's always mad—
but then her puritan sable stole's approved by
most who have authority. In truth she is not really bad,
just dangerous to know. A poppet almost. Defy
the Devil, drink so deep you make the welkin ring
is not her style, nor is the rainbow range. Arachnid,
a spinner out of string–alongs, the sort that would bring
anoraks on to the Worldwide Web.
                                    (*And so abide*
New Labour; sweet, sweet dreams).
                                    Perhaps you've seen
it all before. The Older End will tell you that
they have. Electric dust carts come to clean
the tunnel but soon break down. It's what
you say, not what you do that counts. Dont weep
for unity (Queen Mab, equals One Tongue, One Nation).

This Government spends a million on Irving's decoration.

Mandy's Place has style, Jude's sure of that, yet
what exactly is the dominant style she is not
oversure except it's pre–Post–Modern. (You get
what you deserve at *Mandy's Place*.) What rot
there is is dry and yet the walls are such
that when you lick them with your tongue, all
seem mint fresh. They're Dulux gloss. (Reflect, much
thought's gone into the way Designers treat a wall.)

What is design then but a journey through old time
stealing old ideas and sticking them with glue
until they hang seamlessly together? What crime
is there in that? Few things these days are truly true.

Let's now move backwards. In the end nothing can last
for long. We dig for victory, that way construct the past.

"How do you travel backwards?"
                    "Through wormholes. That's one way.
Owen Glyn Dwr did that, or so it's said by ancient bards
who wrote his life in emlyns. Those chroniclers say
the Welshman did not die in Wales, but vanished. Shards
of his loving cup were found on Offa's boundary Dyke,
nail clippings in a hamlet south of Shrewsbury, strands
of his hair at Kilpeck, near the ancient church.
                                        To hitch hike
to the past or future you must imagine that there are elastic bands
propelling you into a hive of wormholes."
                              Now Jude:
"Yes some are blocked with wax. But when the past is real
and in the Millennium Year time–hops are possible. It's a crude
time plan which sets creation on a direct line. Sometimes I feel
that I've been here before, upon this very spot, pure deja–vu".
"I feel the same", said Karen unto Jude, 'but then most do.

Some say that Elvis is alive somewhere. He did not die
at Graceland, pizza on his chops, be–shitten in the loo,
but lives somewhere close to the town of Hathersage, high
in the hills of Hope and Castleton, there still true
to rock–un–roll, he practices riffs on his git–are, and is the soul
of inspiration. Thinking what he's missed he coins new words
for *Hound Dog*. It's plain he's travelled through a wormhole
into Derbyshire to sit beside a well–dressed well practicing chords.

Leastways *Sun* readers say he has and who would doubt
when some have actually seen a fat man stacking cans on shelves
and picking at his spots. Buddha big, he has gone wandering about
the lanes that lead down to the very dell where, true unto themselves
and to King Arthur, a court heard Gawain's tale of the Green Knight
headless, but determined, riding his Meg into the New Year's night."

Judes found a wormhole, now she'll go through it to find her past.
(Karen and the kids will go as well but won't be recognised.) Gone,
they'll find the origins of destiny. Her next breath never is her last
now she has found a wormhole. She's dared and she has won.

"Mortality is boundless," she cries very loud, "so dive
away".
　　　　(In Oxfordshire a rabbit with a watch has almost caught
her as she speeds on past. He offers cake).
　　　　　　　　　　　　　　　　　　　"I'll thrive
without your help Funny Bunny, though I have next to naught".

She's landed on a Greenwich train. "This wormhole's short,' thinks Jude,
"it's only three hours back, that at the very most, that I've back–tracked
onto the Docklands Light Extension looking out for *Mandy's Place*. I'm shrewd
enough to know that. Three hours is little time and yet I'm totally thwacked.'

(Thwacked—She does not say the effing word, for Jude is never crude.)

'I still know where I am. Life is a masque, a comic interlude.'

Canto Four

The Docklands Line

The Bank — Shadwell — Limehouse — Westferry —
West Indian Quay — Canary Wharf — Heron Quays —
South Quay — Cross Harbour — Mudchute — Island
Gardens, these are the stations of the Dockland's
Light Railway.

Ram, Karen, the children and Jude travel on the Docklands Light Railway looking at Winos, feisty girls and wondering about the significance of mobile phones and the status of people who do not use them.

She's on a train. It's nine o'clock and yet a Wino has got
on and sits beside her. A stream of consciousness that
is all his own swamps forth and floods her space. It's hot
and therefore his rambling is unfocused, all is passion. What
is his origin? That's hard to say. Glasgow is a theme
but so's the Desert War, El Alamein, and an eighth army.
Also *Nine Graves to Cairo*. "His is not a modern dream",
she thinks. A traveller says aloud, "Yon bugger's barmy".
"What did Rommel say," the Wino asks?

                    At times it seems his brain
has penetrated into history. His hive of memory has broken down
as cul–de–sacs appear; these blocked off wormholes. It is a strain
to listen long. His times are out of joint. Hopeless yet not a clown
"There's your answer", he bawls out and points a finger to the sky
as if he sees a General and lost legions.

                      Never ask a Wino, "Why"?

"My name is Ramsey and don't forget it", that into the air.
And who could could forget a name delivered with such
passion. The Bible says this Wino has a place, some share
in God–time, has mortality, but does not say how much
he has. That's why he shouts continuously. Both latitude
and longitude, confirm that name. "I'm Ramsey. Oh forget it."

We're tested on the Underground. It's not with gratitude
the beggars take the pennies that you throw. They've wit
enough to see you feel a twinge of guilt, that's why
they smile upon loose change but if—observe—you throw
a silver coin they will not notch the smile up to a laugh. Coy
glances will get thrown at you but little else. They know
you can afford it. Ignore them, let them simmer in their stew.
To them you are a trick, a John. But what are they to you?

Ram Bhajam watches all from three seats back,
his Oxo box upon his knee, his trinkets stowed
inside his poacher's pocket. He thinks the tick–tack
of the train a modern mantra. The rich and proud
who do not hear this prayer are in great trouble. He does
not speak to Jude but watches her and thinks upon
the Lady Parvati, Lord Siva's consort. A thought goes
through his head but's barely processed.
                                        "In three is one."
That is the thought. "So three meets one."
                                        He gives a little smile.
He thinks about the way that rivers merge far out to sea.
A molecule of Thames, one of the Ganges, another of the Nile
will meet somewhere. All matter merges so. *What Is* will always *Be*.
What Is is always *Is*. And is the opposite *Is* also truly true.

Believe you me the thoughts of Ram are hubble–bubble stew.

"This train will stop at bumpers. Three will proceed and meet
as one upon a distant shore and beg a boon," his intuition says.
"Always trust that in the end everything comes out tidy, falls out neat.
Duality—Siva and Parvati—has virtues, regeneration comes as life decays"

(*Oxo*: Two circles, symbols, of eternity, each side a cross displayed
to show the target that were aiming at. Symbolism like this will stretch
the mind to breaking point.)
                                And in the Oxo box a gilded astrolabe,
the sort that Chaucer used to teach his son the way to fetch
infinities onto the cosmological table so all could sup there.
Open up to see the strength of the ox is crushed to cuboid form
together with a time machine. Brute strength and ingenuity share
in this box's space. White on red tinplate, almost hand–size, warm
to the touch, just like the tabla Siva plays: is this the drum
which makes the universe pulsate for Kingdoms Yet To Come?

Though life moves on this train, yet sometimes it will stop
and passengers alight. Some to the flesh pots go, others to their
homes, to mothers or to children and a wife who sews. *Top
−Shop* girls who have next to naught to lose, and less to share,
move off along Canary Wharf, their destination is some
bank or other. All life is here. Masons with leather cases
and black ties offer travellers peppermints. They do not come
to study Fermat's final Theorems but show their paces
(up to the third degree) upon a chequered floor. Their world
is black and white.
                    Beside them Pole Dancers; happy lasses
on the surface, but actually cynics whose legs get curled
around passion posts as they gyrate.
                                      The middle and the lower classes
travel on his train. Pythagoreans, they will choose
to balance all on black/white squared hypotenuse.

And at the back a woman with two kids. One lies
upon the seat, head nestled in the mother's lap,
one hand hangs down. Another, a small boy, looks wise
beyond his years. He is the first−born so won't nap
the day away, for like all of that sort, not only will he watch
his ps and qs, he'll watch each one upon the train. He knows
his place today but one day he will speak. We'll catch
his words and recognise their relevance.
                                         As life goes
by Jude takes no note of them. They are the background
of our journeys, passengers who hold no interest,
the ones who dont deserve a second glance. Their sort abound
on every train.

               Sleepers move over railway sleepers, for rest
is natural here. When dozing all she values will float way off;
insular, just when her dream−man steals a kiss she'll cough.

As it moved upon the Docklands Line the carriage swayed from side
to side and hicupped over points. On each side Roadways in the Sky.
These balconies of flats give a perspective on architects. "To hide
the working class away," they'd said, "we've filed them high
in tower blocks but let hang their flimsies out on plastic string;
for it's well known they piss in lifts."
                                    These flatlets with poor locks
and window grills, crowd to the line through Poplar, Wapping and bring
poverty close up the Wharf, to Heron Quays, to West India Docks.

The trains Jude travelled on to Leeds weren't like this one,
those seemed they're done a shift upon the Silkstone seam,
they were so dirty. The Docklands Extension carriages shone
for each was of the very best there was in transport. A dream
train almost. Designed by top designers, by sophisticates, its livery
came as white and red and blue, its customers travelled fast delivery.

She's sitting quiet upon the train though taking in the sights,
her girl's asleep, the boy alert. What simmers in the fry–pan
of her mind? The usual bits of trivia and small junk that rights
the ballast all brains own when we get high on urban
splendour. Just when she thinks, "Canary Wharf is like the palaces
the Babylonians built so they'd out–do the Cities of the Plain,"
her mind returns to domesticity.
                                    She then retraces
all her journey back to Castleford. Through ballast we keep sane.

She trails through all the homes she's had: First one the back
–to–back that she once bought with Dave. Her second home,
the one in Richmond Street that lacked a buffer garden, it lacked
a shower as well, but had some special features; chrome
knights on each side of the grate.
                                    At Shadwell a man threw her a kiss.

In Leeds, just for the present, she lives upon a balcony like this.

Karen. 'Oh to be Juliet again and speaking to a star;
young, vigorous, a virgin all in white and scarce fourteen,
else be an Abyssinian damsel with silver dulcimer seated far
away upon a promontory singing into a Westerly, keen
as the hurricane that on the *Cutty Sark* fills a mizzen sail
and drives all pregnant home to England; to be that
girl again.'
       Then at a whisper: "My destiny's to fail and fail
again. Small opportunities get wasted. Tell me, what
good times, where and why they've gone away. Three faces
of my mother Eve are washed away today with tears.
My bed is candy sheeted. I sleep in a man's shirt. The places
that I wish to see I'll never see. Look at me. The years
have not been kind, my neck is scrawned and though I am not more
than thirty–two I'm quite threadbare. Yes, yes I am the poor."

A young lass sits behind her book. She is the sort you'd often see
on trains, nibbling sarnies from a paper bag . You think, "An onion short
of a Ploughmans," on first encounter. A slacko she might seem to be
when first observed yet really quite the opposite. She is the sort
you'd best look to. A floor girl at the London Stock Exchange,
a calculator of the heaviest of sods and odds. Accurate
to four decimal points are her share prices, her stocks as well. The range
of intelligence that her brain grasps is awesome. She can state
the fall on the Hang Sing and the Dow Jones as it occurs, can test
Marks, dance the night away following the Footsie, know that all is for the best
as long as Sterling waltzes on and feels secure. She has an interest rate
that makes the pulse race, understands you let both State and skate
fast fry before filleting and operates like that. Suffice it here to say;
upon the tracks around the Wharf she knows the quickest way.

Jude watches. The way the woman picks her teeth is quite distinctive
she bares them, rolls her tongue along her lower gum. She's shut
her eyes the moment when her nails go in. Feline and instinctive,
therefore every act is ultra–chic and fashionable. Jude's gut
feeling says she is a watcher for small prey. Her eyes look down
on artificial nails, her hair is Sassoon, or the *Matinee Idol*. She
is the *She who men obey*. She travels down from Town
to look for men. Oh yes siree this girl is chic because she's free.
Free to make decisions. Free to speculate and also free to choose
though only when the price is right. In leisure time she'll dance
with all–sorts, but in the day shes free to earn. Shell not lose
out on liberty for she loves a fulsome life. Free to take a chance
she's never worked the Tescos' tills. But will she go a bridge too far.

The logo on her bag of crocodile, in embossed gold, reads *Jaguar.*

Her face is *Sunny Peach* by *Blush*, upon her wrist a watch
with an expensive strap of platinum. (Dante on the bridge
looking at Beatrice saw a vision such as she.) Her native patch
is Muswell Hill. Each morning just for exercise along a ridge,
a long time since a railway line, she'll look towards the City.
There, through haze, she'll see Canary Wharf.
                                        That's why the pull
of romance brings her daily to this wayward train. Don't pity
her her vision. She is as sure as she is beautiful.

Jude looks her up and down. 'Clearly from some wonderworld.
She looks like Shera, He–man's playmate, she whose high disdain
destroys convention and lets a woman breathe, she who's hurled
the sparring stick at Skeletor to make it very, very plain
she would not die just yet. She'd watched it as it curled
in a wide arc, hit him upon the shin (Boomerang) and then
returned.
            If I was her,' quoth Jude, "I'd never pause and count to ten."

A rasta lass reading a book on Proust (her hair
hangs down as dreadlocks, like the wool that's used
to make a clippy rug) sits opposite. She takes great care
with her appearance. In her the East and West are fused;
no one can tell the twixt from t'other. A meridian line
does not exist for her; a real Queen of Sheba she;
one who will always see Solomon as an equal; fine
hands and pastel finger nails. At a talk on cultural diversity
you'll find her sitting central. At thirty–five,
PA to a Lloyds' name, she's clever, has a PhD
(in fact she's several). The type who types, she's learnt to thrive
most anywhere. Around her index finger in finest filigree
a golden ring. In every way a girl of quite distinctive style
for she has seen both poles, seen both the sources of the Nile.

The Islamic girl sitting across the gangway has on those
children's boots which flash. Around her head a simple scarf
in white but on her wrist a Spice Girls' Watch. She chose
to wear a business suit but over it a burqa. More than half
English she has lived only in two places, in Saudi, (in Rabat)
then Halifax. Her father is a Bradford millionaire.
Something in assurance is her Dad. He has a silken hat.
Kaz Ismail is his name.
                        She has a secret she'll not share
with anyone. The site she wants to see before she dies
isn't Muslim Makka but the Ganges at Varanasi in full flood.
The river starts as a trickle on an icicle then, in a surprise
of natural goodness, a cute wee stream appears. It's good
but then like her it's pure of heart and innocent. (Think
then on Allah and on his beneficence.) Water is a powerful drink.

"Surely a moving train of feisty lasses." Jude says this phrase out loud,
"Dedicated, romantic but ambitious. This three–some is a trinity
of what is best in multi–cultured Britain. Just three and yet a crowd
of swirling Dervishes couldn't distract them. More's the pity
that our nation can't have more."

(Statistically we get older by the day,
so on most trains there usually is a travelogue of pensioners. The smell
proves that conclusively, the sweet smell of our humanity's decay
disguised by Yardleys seeps everywhere. But why that is, is hard to tell.)

'And I'm one of the girls. Like them I'm confident, like them I've style.
Of course I curry flavour, second guess, but know what life is for.

Upon my fingers are three sacred stones; opal, amethyst and emerald, a prial
of brilliants which brings to me good luck. At night upon my brow I draw
a bindi, my third eye, also Vishnu's stripes. I'm something you cannot clone.
I am unique,' said Jude, "I'm proud of place, just lack a mobile phone.'

(Men best beware of girls who're on a train and have a mobile phone
for they are in command. At home a father snores, a mother cooks,
but is in instant contact. Tele–communication sets the tone
for chance encounters, and puts all into context. Such never looks
across the chimleys to the place where Dodi's tomb fast rises
opposite the Isle of Urbane Dogs, such has never had
the thrill of Sancho Pansaring out alone so nothing surprises
her for she's in touch with Mam, in instant touch with Dad.

Tap in a code, then enter in eleven digits and domestic bliss
floods fast towards you. They never are alone but come alive
the very moment that the mobile rings (Bring, bring). Nothing is amiss
in households where daughters such as these can ring and give
both latitude and longitude. Like Shera, sophisticated never crude,
they know just where they sit or upright stand; and so does Jude).

She places her small purse upon her ear. She lacks a mobile phone
but having style will not admit that single fact to anyone.
It easily is best to be snug and quiet at home, or else alone
in Cas, than have folk think, who live longside, you cannot con
your way around.
                    As she purrs in the ring she lets her stare
seem inward, almost blank, so that an honest man might think her
shares had fallen as the Han Sing sank or else a rare
Ming Vase had crashed. A dress of black shows that care
and sense of purpose easily rest on her. A phone without a cord,
that is a modern miracle — most things are when driven by a chip.

Just before the final stop the station's Mudchute. One word.
Mudchute! Two nouns conjoined —
                            Jude thinks, 'Harlot's Whip
also two nouns but separate. In Harlot's Whip there is a tad of space
between possessive *s* and *w*. Linguistically it's one with *Mandy's Place.*'

Canto Five

The Corner Shop

Half a pound of tuppenny rice,
half a pound of treacle,
thats the way the money goes,
pop goes the weasel.

To pop means to pawn. *A weasel* is a flat iron. This nineteenth century rhyme suggests that if money is spent on luxuries and inessentials then, in the end, someone has to pay.

Jude looks across at the Dome and wonders if this really is Mandy's Place and then locates the cornershop where Ram has an attic flat.

Descending from the train she trails along the river side
then stands and looks across the water. "Canaletto saw
the Thames from here, I have the postcard. Boats, a wide,
low vista, slopes and a shallop moving to the southern shore
taking John Harrison to the Observatory. He'll talk about *Haitch One*
with Halley, how to measure longitude, and that's for sure.

A craftsman he. Born near to where I live. At Foulby close on
Nostell his nativity. No theorist Harrison; his Maths weren't pure.
Like Christ he was a carpenter and cut his stops and cogs from
lignum vitae. Hard, not needing grease, that wood lasted from then to
now. Day dreaming I will sometimes think about the spartan room
he worked in then; chisels, a plane, a vice and tiny lathe. A true
pragmatic scientist, moving by increments, in perfect mastery,
he found his longitude, and that way he tamed the sea."

She walks along the promenade; A Golden Mile. "Standing there
I will see, against this autumn grey, the elegance of its contours.
At Mandy's Place I'll recognise design and come to share
the thrill Gadhafi felt when looking on his tent." Hours
of travelling to and fro both on her feet and in
her head, have tired young Jude. "I'm fair flaked
out, and that's for sure," she says into the air. "Sin
so you would be sinned against but not when quaked
with tiredness."
              Upon the river walk two kiss. "That's nice," she thinks.
"Perhap's they're lovers, respected man and wife, who take
a stroll before they go into those modern flats. No greasy sinks,
or peeling stair—well, grimed tiles or last year's tide—mark. A flake
of damp won't fall onto their Danish Bacon or the egg, for in there.
all is minty fresh. Insulated from our world, they do not need to care."

Upon their entrance door; *And will be prosecuted.*
That black Helvetica on white — a forward font, bold,
is the font that speaks its mind.
                              "These homes were parachuted
in by foreign architects," thinks Jude. 'Perhaps they hold
their own and yet in every way they're alien. Those who trespass
here will not be welcome. I'd best move on. Fierce dogs
will set on me, this is the Isle of Dogs. *Thou shall not pass*
the litany of these flat dwellers. Yet who are they? Cogs
inside a World Wide Web which holds the East and West
to ransom? Very possibly. Financiers who walk Canary Wharf and
stray upon West Indian Quay need to be watched. The best
ones are dishonest, the worst, elegant and purest evil. England,
though a land worth fighting for in normal times, is in a doldrum.

Ma, pa, dha, ni. Is history always played upon an ancient drum?

Jude looks across the water, "A stately pleasure dome,'
she thinks, 'majesty brought to waste. Each day of toil
comes to an end. *There Is No Place Like your Home.*"

She turns into herself. "Face it Jude, this Dome is not your style
but since it's there you'd best be drawn to it. You sought it out
as *Mandy's Place.* But is it really so? Elegance does not shower
its goodness down, this is the Wasteland, for round about
is desolation; a gas work's silhouette, chimneys of a power
station, wrecked garages, hoardings, unfinished walls.
                                                          Piss
merchants brought me here. They've had me for a chump,
have that cool lot. I came down from the North to look at this.
It's hype that's all around, not elegance. I'm a daft lump,
been sold a puppy dog. This *Mandy's Place* is an illusion.
I will not pay the entrance fee if all I find's confusion.'

Well past the flats, Jude sees a corner shop. In some top
room a radio plays a raga, while on high, inside an upper floor
she hears the Kathak ankle bells. Aloud, "Bells tune this shop."
It's on that upper floor that Ram lives and studies Hindu Law.

Resembling young Aladdin's Cave, this shops a treasure trove
of jars and thoughts upon philosophy. Delhi sweets, '*What,
Or Who Are You*' (That typed on card). Tikka massala. *Love
Thy Neighbour As You Love Yourself.*
                              "A hard one that,"
thinks Jude, "most that I know have learnt to hate
the individual and only look into the Law of Averages."

She hears the drum she heard when, just a mite too late,
she'd stood upon the riverside.
                              At Varanasi, sages
in saffron gowns, and Sadhus, funereal with matted hair,
make for the old stone steps. Best not make nice
distinctions about past, present, future; all are present; simply share.
As Heraclitus said: "We cannot step into a self same river twice."

In Greenwich Ram holds the tabla in his knee:
Sing it Yorkshire Jude: *Sa, ri, ga, ma, pa, dha, ni.*

Ram's mother keeps this store for selling those essentials
that you find you need when each place else is closed, is shut.
The three amp fuse, the bathroom plug, also academic credentials;
all are here. Someone's carved into the door jamb *The Butt
Stops Here.*
                  'There is a hint of accuracy here but not
so very much.'
                  (The Latin tag, *Emporium*, is much the better word
to use on Empire shops, for they're the butt of commerce. The rot
that undermined this Eastend store is dry, and yet the jewelled Sword
of Justice lies upon its counter.
                              "To pare justice from a cheese
is a profundity," Jude thinks. "We're justifiers. When locals pay
in Ibro heads we give them beads and call it Commerce. The *please
and thank you* of the West, that con is finished. On say—
so from Islamic Banks all lose their interest. Best make a full stop
when this happens.
                  This store is Shrilekha's corner shop.

And in an attic, underneath the roof, a quadrant and a telescope.
Also a watch and Woolworth's calculator. These are the tools
that Ram uses when he works hard at his trade. His scope
is infinite but then he studies an eternity. Those fools
who say astrology lacks grains of common sense should think
on Ramas craft, think of his history and of the five careers
of which he is a master.
                              Ask him how old he is. He'll wink
and show five fingers.
                              Fifty, or five thousand years?
Upon his astrolabe these words: *The aim of this object
is that something may be left of us, for we know that
we do not live forever.* Engraved below the maker's name.
                                                            Correct,
Mohammed Kahali—that is the name—Here You Live On. For what
you've left us is the Astrolabe, an instrument of beauty, logic and fine
craftsmanship which leads us on to Harrison and the Meridian Line.

Jude too, a long time since, had straddled time, though not a God.
At Cleethorpes with her Gran and Pop, she'd walked
from Humberston all along the sea strand looking for odd
stones and fragments of small bone. To her they talked
about Creation. Her granddad said that on the shore
are serious clues and hints of how we came to be: grass
shadows, footprints, ammonites;
                                        And then she saw
something different; three metres long a three inch strip of brass.

"That's the Meridian Line," Pop said, "it stretches all the
way to Greenwich Town. Go straddle it".
                                              That's what she did. "Fine.
One foot goes East, the other West. You're free
of prejudice when you stand above that brussen line.
East and West are close. It cleaves to make a unity
of place, and time and theme, it holds notions of infinity,

of order, makes positioning possible. We come to know
our place through measurement. The stars are of little use,
in sussing longitude; though some can help. Clocks show
us where we are, not sums and galaxies. Degrees and obtuse
angles get to us and give some sense of place and presence."

Pop was self taught, a natural scientist who could not pass
along without a comment. He had the well–honed sense,
called common–sense, a sense found in the working class.

John Harrison too had common sense. He saw that wood
had natural grease. He studied woods then cut each cog
from fragments of an oaken keel. Later, when he could,
bought lignum vitae to replace old oak.
                                        Vegetable oil can clog
a moving part, holds dust and can expand, produce a variable.
No good if you would measure time or make a second stable.

Consider this; the Meridian line will pass through the very table
Rama sits at, between his knife and fork, right through his plate.
Like Hari–Hara, a deity born from two men, Rama is able
to recognise the boundaries that are set, able to state
implicitly the point where Siva starts and Vishnu ends,
also where the West meets East. This talent is his primary art
for though he looks for unity, the mantra which sends
forth each cosmic truth contains discord. We do not start
off with lies but a Big Bang,
                                Gods, he knows, follow Creation
they do not mother/father it; they never are first cause
but come long afterwards, dramatic creatures of sensation
they are heart beat, anvil, hammer. Theirs are the laws
of rhythm; free willed they are ridiculous and sublime
in the same breath, but then the Gods can straddle Time.

The Hindu Gods can always straddle time, they also can create
a second's second chance and make it seem decades. Gods toy
with time, stretch and pull it, for they have the simple wish to state
they are ridiculous by breathing life into themselves. That's why
Ganesha is so loved but also laughed at (or is it laughed with).

Hindus love the fat lad with the elephants head and always smile
as they approach with garlands. Consider this, all men who give
an inch can take a foot, most Indic Gods will generally take a mile.

Back to the shop.
                    Behind the till small postcards with the brand
name *Bollywood*: Siva with Parvati, Krishna with his flute. (New
mothers, and old crones; virgin's sweet and lush as shrikand
responded once to Krishna's touch.)
                    Jude: "Now theres the cue
Krishna awaits everywhere. You cannot ask, 'Where do I stand'?
of Krishna.
                    Have I free—will or is all Karma, is all clearly planned?"

The counter is a painted pasting table strengthed with steel struts
Jude eyes it up and down. Now she'll philosophise.
                    "The cure
to end all cures is economic growth through mini—business. She who puts
her trust in this will never perish but have everlasting life and that's for sure.
It says so in *The Second Thoughts Of Chairman Mao*. I'll buy from here.
I'll buy a tin of *Batchelor's Beans* and a glossy *Woman's Own*,
also *Nudes and Gardens* from the high top shelf. The truth is, do not fear
competition but inwardly invest. Plan productively. *Home Alone*
will not get sold to those who lack a video set."
                    And then she saw
the books. They were not ranked by subject but grouped in shades
of blue: Wedgwood, Thatcher, Baby—Bumkins—Blue, azure, raw
lapis lazuli, and that batch of sky—blue blue used nine decades
since to make a sailor's shirt.; the Royal Blue—that used by Spode—
also the Ang—Sax—Eng—Lit—Crit—blue that scholars know as woad.

Upon the highest shelf a special book. Jude stood upon her toes.
Though once Nile Blue its cover had gone brown and smelled the way
that paperbacks will smell if damp. (Remember this she chose
to take it down and look. Old things hold interest, smelling of decay,
smell captivates.)
It told of Dodi's ancestry, though next to nought
is that. He had no quartering, no lozenges of heraldry
emblazoned forth his heritage as on a tomb. Though caught
inside the trap of poverty Al Fayed knew a way to free
the family—Groceries. Not genealogies painted in blue blood
but book keeping kept their family. Debit not *Debrett*, the tool
the father used to build a Knightsbridge Empire Store. He could
make a load of money selling spice.
(Was Dodi just the fool
who followed on as second of a line. Would that be true?
And if it was, was it exactly that the Princess loved and knew?)

He was no fool, Dodi simply lacked a GCE or two.
Indulged, his was a life of sex, of drugs and rock–un–roll,
before he met the Princess. He'd snort, raunch and do
the things that rich kids do before they courted. But now; scroll
down the menu of a life like his. Upon the hard disk youll find
gem stones.
(Consider: His servants liked him. A good start
that for servants see a man before he's showered. Kind
to children and small animals? Always. He had part
ownership of a flock of grouse therefore the desire
to kill for pleasure never crossed his simple mind.
Talented? He got an Oscar once for *Chariots of Fire*.
What was it Jesus said, "Seek and you will find.")

The book had *Di and Dodi*: Love engraved upon the spine. Few
titles state a case quite that direct. You know that's true.

Upon the jacket of this book, a map, not of the universe
but of the streets she stands among. She sees the shop;
signed with the letter O. "That's for the Great Om." A tantric verse
shaped in her mind.

(*Om* for the Hindu is the moment of full stop,
the wisp that stands between *harlot* and her horse–tail *whip*,
between Cuttee and her Sark, twixt Canary and its Wharf but is not
found in Mudchute.)

Jude does not act but counts to ten. She takes a grip
upon herself and so prepares. Like Ram she will think first. The rot
has not set in and *Om* upon the cover makes it clear it's time to slip
into the present. The Tunnel is a wormhole. Now she will go
through to meet the here and now. Walk on to see the Clippy Ship,
the harlot with the tail of Meg, Dodi's Dome, the show
to end all shows, embrace the brace *ignorance and apathy*.

Because she's young Jude neither knows or cares, so's on the Quay.

Canto Six

The Nation's Loss

"Does the deceased have any aliases?"
Standard question put by the Registrar of Births and Deaths

Jude listens to Zarathustra (an alias) and meets Mills and Boon.
They talk about the death of Di and Dodi and explain the plot of
The Nation's Loss.

Eight metres on, with mangy blankets round their knees,
three chufflings squatting in a row, a crown
of thorns is balanced on each head.
                              "Change please,"
they say to Jude as she walks by. She stops, kneels down
beside the first. "What is the change you need," she's asks?
He draws his dog in very close until its stinking breath
well mixes with his own. "What change," again? "What tasks
will you perform for change?" He goes as pale as death.
She asks him yet again. "What is the change you think you need
to change this worthless life?"

                    Come off it Jude he does
not give a chuff for change. He simply needs to read
of fortune in the stars. That done he'll don his dancing shoes
and tip–tap round. Give him choice and see him fail to choose.
He does not ask for change, he just wants brass for booze.

These chufflings are life's drolleries, jokers who when time is up
move from their pitch and gad about for laughs. These women
and this man, there's three of them, once passed the loving cup
of full employment, now proper jobs are rarely found. When
life has passed you by, and few need serving, you become the Give–
–An–Inch–And–Take–A–Yard brigade, mood changers, folk who range
about to form opinions. An underclass who choose to live
upon the steps of High Street banks; that's why they ask for change.

And this one's Karen's Man, the wight you've met in Canto One.
He"s in disguise. The Giro he picked up in the P.O., in Ropergate,
long since has disappeared. It's spent, it's well and truly gone,
there is no trace of it, yet he still has the sarnies and the plate
he'd sneaked the morning when he tiptoed out and left her dry and high,

"Harken," he cries aloud, "Observe the Dome — but don't ask why!"

He has an alias, he's Zarathustra now, for East meets
West in names like Zarathustra. Girls say its really cute;
not those who know their Nietzsche. The cobbled streets
of Munchen heard that name on Kristallnacht. "The route
it took was strewn with glass. He's problems, has this lad."

He hasn't for he'd seen the name upon a wall in Leeds
to sign a Band of Supermen, a band of heavy rock. "Not bad—
just feckless" tattooed on their arms. What sort of man needs
this to brand himself. Why must he take a name that hes seen
written on a wall?
          That's hard to comprehend. Here
in the West a name means naught. An actress–has–been
called *Patricia* Rock spawned a thousand Pats. Beer
names are sometimes used. Tetley Wrigglesworth and Bass
Profundo, both play in the Sunday League in Leeds.
                                  A lass

in Heckmondwike's Sam(antha) Smith. High class
you think at first but when you recognise the boozy joke
her Dad had made on when Christening her you pass
her on the other side and snigger.
                      Her lovers never spoke
her name for fear of giggling. "I love you sweet Sam
Smith," dripped from the tongue—and then they'd laugh.

Sam's ending? Happy. She moved to Birmingham.
A lesbian. Michel(le)–Butler became her better "half."

In Featherstone there is an Elvis fan whose name is Plews,
a dominant type, he named his first born *Blue Suede*.
(Up in the hills of Hathersage a fat man hears this news,
pauses as he stacks a shelf of *Snickers*. That naming's made
his day).
             Native Americans choose a fish or bird or beast
name for they empathise with nature; five years at least

before the name is given.
            The name he chose had antecedence.
Zarathustra–Zoroaster–Zardushi, call him what you will,
had lived in Persia when Buddha was a boy. From thence
he'd travelled every highway singing loud the *My Way* Song. A still
intelligence enflamed by fire informed him. Scratting round about Tehran
he'd found philosophy. He said that all was sand, the objects of desire;
women, wine, and that selfish song, were all illusion; for each one a span
of years is set. "*Renounce*" he said, "Go worship all there is with fire".

Zarathustra—the origins of his alias did not concern him—
for any thing's better than Dave or Karens Ex.
                        "What's in a name?"
he's asked himself. Jake Zarathustra now. He'd chosen it on whim
but having done so he will stick with it. Don't take the blame
for every alias that you have. Remain secure and do not give a damn.

He spoke with clarity on his philosophy "I simply act because I am."

Thus spake up Zarathustra. He stated *La Philosophie Existentiale*,
as then he saw it, to those who'd listen.
                        "Life is playing a part
you have invented for yourself. Having aliases, showing essential
invention, knowingly creating a persona, that's better than Sartre,
Left Bank Learning, *Gauloises Disque Bleu*, Modern Art
and L'Ecole des Paris, conversation at Deux Margot
(Saint Germain–des–Pres across the square) with part –
time philosophers, better than Simone, better far than Cocteau.

Thus Zarathustra: "I've style and culture, am the first of three
who sits upon the pier, is looking down the Thames towards
the Isle of Dogs".
                        Jude ponders, "His interest in philosophy
is slight. He don't know much, just knows the things he likes. Few words
will cross his lips to challenge me. He seems simply to speculate
but his logic is limited; he's poor of reason, cannot calculate".

Two women shared his bed–room space upon the Mitre step. They seemed
happy with each other. "Writers for sure," Jude thought. They chatted
on in a literary way settling old scores. Said who'd creamed
who and why in 1958, that sort of thing.
                                        Teapot cosy but hatted
in black fur, clothed tip to top, like femme fatales, in Russian mink,
they said that long ago they had gone culture touring and had hit
some high spots in Belarus with Barstow–Braine. (*The Kitchen Sink
School of Novelists*, their heavy period.) They were the soul of wit.

(A literary illusion: Jude's dad had played for Wakefield Trinity when
David Storey played and wrote *This Sporting Life*).
                                        "Do you thrive
on gossip?"
            The Scots one smiled. "I'm sure that you must ken.
John is Braine dead. Barstow's gone to Bronteland, to live
in Haworth town."
                 The other gave the look that regularly kills.
"You'll know us well, She's Mistress Boon and I am Mrs Mills."

"Yes, I am Mistress Boon. When times are really bad each fills
a Basildon and sends it to a publisher. We make ends meet."

"Our books sell well in China and in the Middle East," said Mrs Mills.
Her friend, her Tweedledum, replied, "Because they have neat
endings they're loved around Setzwan and in Hong Kong,
Old Red Guards from Futures Brokers borrow them. The Han Sing
rises to meet their popularity. That's because we celebrate strong
sensual plots played out in paddy friends. Sweet, but never sour, the ring
of truth is ever heard. Boy does meet girl in Canton and in the typists' pool
girl does meet boy. Sex is never first night raunching. Decorum Est
our motto from the first.
                         Personally I'd rather make raspberry fool
than have one as a hero. The girl I'll always choose will test
the boy, will finger flirt with him but if his hands should stray
beyond her knee, we'll cross him from our Basildon. Him in? No way".

There is a type of woman likes a right big man. They
suit their style for they are always oven warm. They think
at pulse rate speed, are fun, rarely adulterous, in play
hippopotamus slow, they surface late, wander to the sink
yawning and slap cold water onto roly–pols before—sweet tea
in a pint pot—they go back to their duvets. Invariably they delay
love making time for they need massive kip.
                                        "Agree
with me," says Karen, "such men are fun. They never pay
their round, I will concede, yet all–in–all they come free
and very easy. Every day's a joy, life one spending spree."

Jude's ideal man would come from Pomfret, have a bum that's just
two handfuls. Karen's not like that. Though never raucous, never loud,
her wants in every way are massive like the universe. "Trust
a man who has a bottom like the top most reaches of the cloud
surrounding Ursa Major." Her eyes go glazed. "Treasure trove
are such big men. Crush huggers, they deserve my love".

Karen's hero is Dolph Lundgren, he starred in *Rocky Four*
but is best known as *He–Man* in Warner Bros 95 release
of *Masters Of The Universe*; blue eyed and to the core
fjord fresh. "Wonders like he," she said, "Should never cease."

(These small particulars as you know don't drift the plot
along, they're there to shed some light on Karen's needs
and personality. Psychology matters in Eng. Lit. Crit. not
narrative. Footnotes also matter.
                                She who regularly reads
The Guardian, or the literary reviews, will understand.
Fashioned poems with plots and structure are very rare
these days. As are fantasy poems about planned
parenthood. It's performance, performance everywhere.
Small men with microphones voices, Rule OK, not fine
honed ghazels; Persian poetry with no story–line).

Among our writers Mills and Boon are very rare. Patriots
in all things. The colour of their blankets—powder blue. To wean
us back to English Literature is their cause. The sans culottes
(peasants without drawers) who sat around the guillotine
and knitted woollen clouts, had read their type of book. Voltaire
had used their timeless plots in *Candide* when telling us about
the love his hero had for Cunegonde. And yet they didn't care
for him. *Too Frenchified.* "Harold Robbins he could shout
the odds, although a Yank," said Boon. "Micky Spillane
writes well but for real craft I'd always choose the aloof
prose of Virginity Woolf. The passage in *Orlando* where the plain
nurse gets the Indian doctor bears the ring of truth"
"Inside the house of Literature sound structure is the test
of books, not Booker panelling. Sound plots are for the best."

"It's that which makes yon *Juliet and Romeo* a real poor read,"
said Mistress Mills. Her partner took the theme "It's a poor play
for sure," said Mrs Boon. "Take the ending. There's little need
to kill them off at all. To kill them off in such a sloppy way,
that's a disgrace. The messenger could come in time and
save the star–crossed. It's not as if the Stratford Bard
can't make a happy ending. Dwellers on sylvan land
kiss best in leafy Arden, so Forget–Him–Not. He's a hard
act to follow, that's if he sticks to Windsor or to Warwickshire.
Why choose to gad about in Tuscany or else in a small part
of Europe that he does not know? Authors all have the desire
to set their scenes upon the God–grouped Himalayas, the real art
is modestation and constraint. The skill is not to set the scene
in fair Verona but in a cul–de–sac close on to Golders Green".

"Yet I'll say this, in life some facts will shadow fiction. Reason
will go awry; sentiment and sophistication mix. That's when a clump
of cliches come to rule okay."
                              Boon: "This story starts in the season
of silliness At the time when cub reporters raunch and seek to triumph,
to cap each others tale, no one was doing much.
                                              The Lady Di
had come to Paris with her Muslim beau. They got on very well
although she was a Spencer and he; he was a grocer's boy
called Dodi."
              "And did he love her?"
                                     "That's really hard to tell.
He fancied her and that's akin to love or so the glossies say.
He had a sapphire ring in a black box, there was a distant date
when they would wed, (or so it's said.) He'd had his way
with her. (that's said as well), but he'd still marry. Eleven; it was late
(And so to bed. Sweet dreams.) An underpass beneath the river
and a car chase. Rat driving hard. Two together, drunk the driver.

They hit the thirteenth pillar (Ill luck for sure). The Seine
passed over them. Below a Fiat speeding forth. It did not
stop. (Fiat Uno) Postillions on motor bikes. Pike staff plain
police (Bring–Bring). Emergency. (Bring–Bring)
                                              "Was there a plot"?

"Some papers said there was, headlines proclaimed *Conspiracy*."

Mills: "They lived their life for us but now have passed the loving cup
to others. Dodi dead and Diana numb—a survivor in mockery
of pain. Inside her cavities a reservoir of blood was building up".

"Two kissed upon the Bucking balcony. All subjects will.
recall jam tarts and all the pasting tables placed in one long line,
in their street piles; of buttered bread."
                                "Remember her until
Eternity implodes upon its self and latitude falls into a decline."

"Observe six carrying one into a different reservoir of tears.
A guardsman placing his warm cheek up close to hers".

[75]

"And then the flowers. Carnations and roses thrown beneath
hearse wheels as slowly they moved on at steady pace
towards her resting place. Upon the coffin just a simple wreath
from her two boys. (They'd walked in Whitehall.) The black ace
now has trumped the diamonds and the hearts. All falls to disarray."
Jude: "We are small spades and clubs."
                                            "In a tradition and with grace,
they bring her forth with muffled drum. *The Nation's Loss* and a display
of grief that is unique. She lies alone tonight in Spencers' Place."

"There is a Spencer Place in Leeds where young girls bob at men
that pass in cars. They wind down windows to ask "What price?"

"She's on an island at her brother's place. The people curtsey but then
her dignity produced courtesy in *Uz and Them*. The lowered eyes a nice
touch in the repertoire of all who'd watched her. One of the world shakers
she'd passed from us. We the groundlings; The Press the undertakers."

"And what of Dodis tomb? His menfolk washed his body down
and said the Prophet's prayer *O Allah now forgive*. No longer lover,
playboy, favoured son; he had returned to dust. No gown
of silk but three white winding sheets were placed to cover
him with dignity. *Make his grave spacious and grant
him light in it*. The prayer is ended. All men are equal and are
brothers. That is implied at Muslim funerals. Religious cant
is there unknown. They turn upon the west and pray. All share
the knowledge we are dust and earth and unto earth return."

Jude has an insight. Sees a whited sephulcre, a Dome so light
it seems to float on space. Though feckless Dodi will not burn
but rise again to watch the crescent in ascent upon an Arabian night.
That's why he needs a tomb, a spacious place, the panoply of glory.

"Tell me please," Jude speaks direct, "did you two write the story?"

Canto Seven

Heroes and Heroines

Above all, when you come across a molehill, think twice before you jump on it. There are Moles and Femoles living in it—and it took a long, long time to build.

Frank and Allan Brammah   *Margarella, the Moles and the Money Tree* 1985

Conversations take place about nicknames, coalmining communities, important pit families and Al Fayed's relatives.

Beneath her arm Mills holds an ancient leather bag. It has elastic sides
and is so stuffed with Stephensons and Newton notes
it might burst out at any time. Jude: "Which of you decides
the way a plot should tumble forth?"

"That is our craft. Boats
that pass at night and carry heavy cargo, also themes like farting,
get pencilled out immediately. Though not fastidious, we both like well
enough a robust smell, but it is the touch tongue and a hero departing
to "I Love You". It's the quiet hug that sells best. The death of *Little Nell*,
(a soap before its time for sure) has no place in our genre,
and why the Dickens should it. We're here to give satisfaction
and added value, not dwell on the here–after. It's the tendre
brush of satin upon the skin we celebrate. The rest's reaction."

Jude: "Have you a hero or a heroine. Someone, who like a kindly light,
leads you beyond the stunted tree into the Cheddar Gorge of Night?"

"There's such a man," said Mills, "though few will know his name
or work. We know of just one piece. We met him once. Upon the night
that Charles, our Prince, got married to the Lady Di, this man became
our hero. We stood behind him in the Mall and, though tight
packed, we saw him take some scissors out and as Charles bent
to place a kiss on her receiving lips, with subtlety and snip,
snip, snip, he cut it forth from cardboard. Miraculous! It's heaven sent
is talent such as that."

Boon drew the inference. "The harlot's whip
which drives on artists; the thirst for fame, cannot create that man
we watched at work upon his pop–up book."

Before the cheering ceased he had
the cut out safely stowed inside a plastic envelope, and more; the plan
on how to shape the theme."

"He was a paper engineer. If any cut became a tad
misplaced Chas kisses Diane's nose."

"Or he might kiss her ass."

This line from Mrs Mills. Boon was refined. Ms Mills more working class.

"Let's agree, this was a dense crowd, yet he had the class
to scissor in a confined space."
                              "That's Art," said Mrs Mills,
"and that upon the night of nights he'd easily pass
paper engineering GCSE with a starred A and all the frills.

"Miriam," Mills said, "I'm sure our young friend wants to hear
about the love Charles had for Di but lost in Highgrove. Why go
on about our friend and scissoring–against–the–odds. I fear
you'll bore her. Girls do not want this sort of story."
                                        "That is not so,"
said Jude. "I love to hear of wonders and a scissorer who can
come forth to make the welkin ring excites me. One audacious feat
will ever interest me. You say he cut the figures out without a plan
or template. A hero unto me he is for sure. I hate a world where neat
ideas form rows and hold the sylvan landscape in the grip
of order. A real romantic, I wish for wonders. That's why this trip

to London has inspired me so. Where I come from pre–destination
was the theme that held us close together. Everyone was kith and kin
Boys to the pit. We'd a twenty close to my town. Job creation
was not a problem. Self advancing faces were the norm. The Jinn
was in the bottle fifteen years ago".
                              With pride Jude named some
pits. "Fryston, Big K—that stands for Kellingley. Two thousand men
worked there in doom and gloom. Proud productive lads who came
to work for pleasure; that and steps of bread and lard. I recall when
Big Kellingley won medals every month. Dedication, the key
to productivity, was always theirs."
                              She named a fist of others.
"Ledston Not–Much–Luck—a riding shaft by Kippax—Methley
Junction, the Prince of Wales, Shafton Colliery, Back Bill's Mothers,
Normanton and Fryston Seams; the shale between was six foot thick
and perilous. Roof falls common".
                              Karen: "My father rescued Donkey Dick,

the famous Castleford Underman, from under boulder clay
and as he did they sang the *My Way* song. Their singing saved
the bit of life he cared for. That Friday was a sad, sad day.
He left his better part, or least a foot of it, behind but waved
to all as he was stretchered out. Six girls in shawls stood round
and grieved. He was world famous—least ways round there—
was Donkey Dick.
        Each had a nickname or a smell or sound
which made their presence felt. If lacking you took great care
to get one fast.
        Fart Wilkinson. Who needs an explanation
for a name like that? But whys he OBE? A grateful nation
was glad he worked weekends and rarely surfaced at
day time. Rippers on the face worried about the methane gas
that built up when he stayed down over long—but that
is history. If constipated he could light your Davy lamp. In a class
all of his own was Fart. They gave the honour in perpetuity to swell
our local pride. He married Cak Clout Nance, so I've heard tell."

Jude can go on and on when talking of the Good Old Days,
her detail's always interesting, the plot will never over
boil if we stand by to chew this cud.
        "Colliers still sing the praise
of Nance. She had few golden rules. Mobile, she was a rover
in the culinary arts. Once at the Prince she used a hundred
bags to make a single pot of *Tetley's Tea*. The canteen
cheered as it flowed forth and settled. It has been said
she then threw in Dick's khaki shirt for colouring. Queen
of the sarni counter she later still received a commendation
from a big man at NCB HQ. It said *Ich Dien*. "*I serve*"
(the motto of the Prince of Wales but on a mug). Our nation
had bestowed on her that honorarium. Did she deserve
it? Of course she did. We locals need to celebrate each heroine
who creates new arts. By nature she's a genius but benign."

There are some folk who think the heroes of the working class
have serious limitations. They think because the blue and white confetti
that we throw down when Bert weds Gill or Sam weds Samth—the lass
who lives next door—sops to papier mash and their tinned spaghetti
comes laced with cocktail sausages, they lack imagination. They classify
upon a five point scale so do not look for fall–out much below the Bs.
How ignorant and wrong they are to be that mechanistic, for who'd deny
Stephenson, although a Geordie, arose with craftsmanship and ease.

If you would wade into this mess of social mores you'll see real skill
resides in granting nick names. In sending forth a ribald metaphor;
there's literary art. Colliers do not stand on ceremonial. *Willy*, for Will
Shake–speare, two penile images there. Consider and ask why *Two Whore*
Jackson and *t'Old Cock*? Why are most Clarks called *Nobby*?
And *Donkey Dick*; is that a feature of his form or just a hobby?

If you're a daughter in a clan of mining men you know
that *Afternoons* reach down the pit from two till ten,
that *Nights* roll on from gone half nine, you show
affection when you can but most ways can't. But then
the collier's life has compensations. Slack at the grate back
ensures hot water, gran's smalls don't become floor clouts
but are used as bannikers (wide collier pants). A sack
of shale—called *your allowance*—can be thrown at louts
who sing along and bang about. Girls who're on the game
in Spencer Place will sell themselves for coke. Oh there are hosts
of pit tales. There's pillocking and bollocking, recitals of the same
scary story you have heard the umpteenth time about ghosts
who walk old galleries; miners from Fryston and the nether region
making strange faces and gipping; their dirty habits, legion.

Two nieces worked in Woolies on the pick–and–mix. The bright
ones went to study at the Pudding School, for we were close
on Leeds, and there were several in its hinterland. At night
the Yorkshire bus to Royston would be full of them. They chose
to stay at home and not to wander far. More adventurous girls
went off to Loughborough College. Healthy, on their thighs
strong muscles rippled as they ran. Girls like Shera. When curls,
close cropped, lay on the salon floor they would devise
programmes of fitness based upon the splits. They gave
themselves to sport and to aerobatics never unto men,
they smelt of sweat but were not butch or *Brut*. A slave
to golden slumbers? No, rather rising with the lark, running ten
miles around the muck stacks of the Prince Of Wales, so fit,
they never wore a vest of thermal holes beneath athletic kit.

There were other women. They would stand beside the Buttercross,
awaiting charabancs to take them on to Dewsbury and the Pennine Mills.
Heavy woollen lasses each and as they stood they slagged the boss.
Theirs was life lived at the raw of morning frost. There are few thrills
in making shoddy cloth, believe you me. The Pennine weather up in
Halifax is dull and wet, the spinning sheds both damp and grey,
the noise is clatter–chatter. Humid in their humanity each wore a thin
dress underneath her wrap–around and lip read to pass the time of day.

Jude: "I've chatted on too long. It is a fault I share with most
who live restricted lives in an extended family though one that
Dodi Fayed shared with our lot. Sitting making fresh toast
on a toasting fork then passing it to Dad. He was a wonder. What
joy compares with that. Although all Pharaoh–rich each shares
the real joi de vivre of Uncle Kossihaggi. Yes, each one cares.

Jude had an ancient copy of *Hello* so knew about this clan
of Mayfair Egyptos. They were Di's heroes and her heroines,
people who like her were once rejected. Although each man
and woman and child were jack–pot–lottery–rich the sins
of avarice — opal sins and ruby sins — were not irrelevant.
Patrons of the Arts and horses, they'd made their pile
in groceries and armaments; theirs was a constant war on want,
they simply wanted more. To get their way they would defile
the Temples of Commerce. When partying the Lady Di saw how their
cups of tea were laced with whisky and she loved the life;
all was laid back. In one big flash she saw she too could share
her all with exiles from the Land of Ra and Nod. To be the wife
of Dodi that would be fun. Oh yes this Diane was a turning worm.

She starry eyed. She'd join their company. Would join a gun and grocery firm.

Jude: "Back to the scissorer."
                    Mills: "We talked to him that night
about his skill. There is a gallery close upon Trafalgar Square
where cognoscenti go for cappuccino, its called the ICA."
                                        "A right–
on place is that for sure".
                    "Some like its ambience of sitting there
amongst the riff and raff of Art. It is an artists' society
for those who live on grants, on buggery and giving favours.
That's where we heard his tale.
                    He was a northerner, propriety
and sober habit were his bags. A man of grace and flavours.
"Where is he now?"
                    A strange look passed between
them when Zarathustra made the *Peace Be With You*
sign, that simple, silent benediction. Jude thought she'd seen
that sign before. Since elemental it was both good and true
yet no one looked into Jude's eyes, each gave the shy–coy look.

"This is Nick Cooper–Kite, he made the pop–up book."

Jude: "But you are Karen's ex."
                    "Yes and through that understand me.
I have other names as well. These let me croon the *My Way* song. I'm Nick
Cooper–Kite (Design) today. Tomorrow if the Footsie rises *Peat Marwick plc.*
Sometimes I am The Honourable Chas, Grindling Stubbs, Fatso, Spick–
Span, then quite familiar, Burton Suet, Eric Gill, the late
Wynkyn de Worde, Charlie Kunz, Diz Gillespie, Edmundo Ross, Po
Blair, Zarathustra–Zoroaster (what you will), Dave Micklethwaite.

"I know your family" she was relieved. "Are you a Micklethwaite too?"

He: "Only by marriage. I took young Karen's maiden name,
though not her maiden head, upon our wedding day. New
to the marriage vows—I'd never been divorced though claim
descent from sixty six who have—it seemed correct. I grew
through travelling to Loughborough and London; that much for sure."

Jude closed one gimlet eye and looked at him. "Please tell me more."

Canto Eight

The Designer's Tale

'To the celebrated French alienist, Esqirol, is due the signal merit of having discovered that there are forms of mental derangement in which thought proceeds apparently in a perfectly rational manner, but in which, in the midst of intelligent and logical cerebral activity, some insane presentations appear, like erratic boulders, thus enabling us to recognise the subject as mentally diseased.'
Max Nordau, Degeneration, London, 1920.

In which Karen's Ex tells of his love of Loughborough and the Rise and Fall of the Ladybird Empire.

"What happened when you left the town of Pontefract
blue back pack on and money in your poke? With that poor lot
called Karen, you had had your way," said Jude.
                                        "I always act
before I think. A Virgin on the Pancras line urged me. I got
a saver ticket and to the Midlands made my way. Creation
sends forth signals. And then I saw one. A simple sign
said *Brush*. It sat above the Loughborough railway station
in 30,000 volts. That sign charged me. The profane and divine
are always close at hand. The neon sign said simply *Brush*.
I thought unto myself, "You've chosen this or it has chosen you."

Sikhs wave a *brush* above their sacred book. The thrush
found in the hawthorne bush, the speckled throstle who's true
unto itself and sings at the dawn, is music's *brush* with nature; all link!
I saw the sign. All happened in a flash. *Brush!* I did not think.

I acted (Away the lads) I saw the neon sign and ran
The sacred brush of Mr Singh, a hedge of brush wood
and a singing bird, the sign above the railway station. I began
to see how themes converge to make poetic wholes so could
have pondered long.
                        Religion, Nature and the neon sign of Art,
yes all were all there. Would they remain if I stayed on and thought
things over? I thought they might. Success goes to the bold. Part
of the train can never reach the station — the platform is a mite too short.

Sit in the carriage at the back, the one for smokers — men who flick ash
on lap tops, girls with yellow nails — and as the loco slows, watch
how fast they move. With cough and splutter each one makes the dash
to get to Carriage E. They seem to know they must adjust to snatch
an opportunity. Observing them I took my chance. I came up from low down.

Theirs also was my stop. I took up residence in Loughborough town

Of course I knew the place by reputation. Quality socks
to fit the boots and shoes made in Northamptonshire,
the wonderful baji and the vindaloo of *Ko–i–Nor*. Locks
made by Lock and Co, precision locks of safety which require
four keys and serial pass words, ideal to hold close shut
the outside lavy door at night; locks so good that
should you lose a key, although your wife might rave but
you know best, you must remove the scullery wall. What
locks.

(The enlarged kitchens found in Padgett Street were
made because one matron in a well defined subversive act
against her husband Dr. J M Ramakrishna—they'd share
a bed but not philosophy— rose in defiance. I know this for a fact
she hid her key where he would never find it—inside a gardening boot—.
you see he rarely gardened. The women in the street all followed suit.)

Look for modifications in your house design not in the notions
of Austrian architects but in the judgements folk will make
to have a living space that satisfies their needs. Solutions
found in *Jugendstil*, though interesting, are not required.
                                                            Take
from the family for the family cares about the how
and where and why of life so all they offer on design
is worth consideration.
                        Make this your axiom, show
deference to this above all things. On qualities of wine
most proles are hopeless but on the way two rooms will mesh
in with a third they are supremitorio. Not only are they right,
they're Frank Lloyd Wright as well. Home improvement is the crèche
of new creation and central to the good life. Avoid the up–tight
and architectual critique rather accept commands found in the *I–Spy*
Book–Of–Building and yet be sure your tools are ever DIY.

This is Leicestershire's place of prophecy. Before most spoke of *diversity*
of culture Loughborough had it.
Ergo: There is a bell tower like a Bradford
mosque in the town centre which will not play religious tunes. The university
is run by men in track suits not pin stripe. Each one a doer, they say discord
will come if press ups and the Swedish drill aren't practiced on a regular
basis. "The world, as it is understood, will fall apart if we don't daily exercise,"
is what they say. "Avoid the thin and puny, all be spick and spam. Your jugular
vein must be masked by muscle." *Veni* (I came) their motto.
That's no surprise;
the Chancellor and Dean were massive men. The honorary degree they give
is *Master of the Universe* (M. Uni); These academics all get up at five past sunrise
don *Nike* kit plus cap and gown for squash racquets. They live
for Physical Culture before all other cultures. Don't show surprise
on meeting fit fat men, see that sportsmen–academics can never really fail.

"Enough of this," says Karen's ex, "the time ticks on, I must complete my Tale".

"I wandered from the wayward train onto the taxi rank
and ordered a cab with plastic. 'Take me *First Direct* to where
I'll find the very best there is of printed knowledge, a credit bank
of wisdom, take me to the local publishers for I would stare
in constant wonder on publications. It's said that there so many cooks
stir at the stew it's always fresh, that's why they never fail to please the boy
who, though just thinking free, has need of access onto picture books
which are an easy read. Books for his type are now in short supply.

I joined them to publish books about the nuclear family. Janet and John, Rover
Pigeon the cat, Pop, (the aged Grandsire); in apron with white hair, Gran—
a wonder world of people in a lovely hardbound library. *The Lover*
of Lady Chatterley, The Memoirs Of O, Excess, The He–man
Annual, Strip–Tease, Single Mum; books printed with taste for gain,
had no place on our lists.
One page colour, the other printed plain.

Now all's in ruin and I've moved on, yet there I got all knowledge
that I have about the art of pop–up books and populist publishing.
I got it all upon the draughtsman's board, upon that hardest edge
of all, the metalled rule. With mat and scalpel I built the wishing
well from which I drew success. A drawn bucket need not go down.
I drew on bourgeois virtues and high quality graph, thus I cherished
virtue writing regularly every day. Each drawing was my very own
designed and executed all by me. In publishing I truly flourished.

Qualifications—next to none. I was self taught and yet I so
impressed the boss, Old Meister Mann, that he came to agree
to have me there till I was happy ever after. Gold leaf not Day–glo–
golden his enthusiasm. A publishing colossus, yet his respect for me
was *Totale Plus*. Most found him coarse—he'd rage about and shout—
and yet to me he was a gentil knight,
                                        This is how our friendship came about.

When I got to Loughborough, believe you me I was no happy bunny.
Judged in linguistic terms I did not quite fit in. Their complex gyrations
of speech confused me, here the profound balanced with the funny."
They practised alien lingos that brought on palpitations.

In Yorkshire we speak the word *love* because it knits us all together,
In every sentence spoken, eye–ball straight unto another, it is there.
'Whats going off then, love.' 'Rheumatism, love' 'Bad weather
love.' Know our philosophy. In Yorkshire Love conquers Fear.

It was as if when genteel Jesus came across from Galilee
in ancient times to walk the mountains and the hills
of Rippendon. There he blessed the earth and left a legacy.
That gift is with us still. It's Love, pure love. Inside Satanic Mills
where shoddy cloth is made, and women cannot speak just mime,
maybe it is almost lost. But even there it's there some time

it will return for it is love. Also in that dread time, the awkward space
before the last full stop comes galloping, love will come
and, oh so gently, it will lie with you. 'Yes love, yes love'.
                                                    In place
of *love* in Leicestershire and Notts, in house and home,
up–hill down–dale, *love* gets replaced with the sole word *duck*.
'Duck fetch,' 'Duck find,' 'Duck this, duck t'other.' 'A bad cough
duck,' 'This pill will end it all, mi duck.' Miss it, chance your luck.
When our *love* holds to centre stage, a *duck* just waddles off.

It's ever duck. Men with tattoos of Satan on each arm say, 'Mother
duck what's up.' Girls who wait and wonder how their tender breasts
will grow say, 'Give me a ciggy, or else a kiss, mi Duck.' No other
well used words 'cept *the* and *a* compares. Gross heavy weighted beasts
with two backs raunching when they collide say *duck*.
                                                    "Heavens above,"
said Jude, "is duck the word used with force in Lawrence's *Women In Love*?"

Jude: "In Yorkshire the word love is always close at hand."

"Not here, least ways not here right–off. And then it came
as a lovely lady—Lotus Anna Byrd. A one night stand
extended until we two became a pair and took the blame
for each one's faults. "He is like that because she made
him so." Then gradually, "Come as a pair tonight
—And I can tell you duckling how we did!—"the table's laid
for four and you are two, our special guests. The light
will be twelve tall candles, the napkins' Wicklow white,
and Waterford the glass. Come sevenish, we eat at eight."

(Courtesy is Loughborough's watchword. These are not tight
lipped folk from Leicestershire but gentles who will state
their case and hold to it, craftspeople and printers, no pomposity
claimed their days, they moved with more than ample generosity.)

"What was her tale"?
                    "It is not mine to tell. Read your horoscope,
you'll find her there for sure, a Pisces swimming both ways.
I will not speak of her except to say that in the end she couldn't cope.
Marriage, two children, hard work—tiredness always plays
a part when early force is spent—the inevitable
misunderstandings, missed dates, worry upon worry, drift
into the sad slough of despair, the gradual climbing out, a stable
husband beckoning from a quiet house in Linden Lea, their rift
was healed with scar tissue; his hearth again became her fire."

"Was she untouched?" asked Jude
                    "Don't be so young , don't be naive.
How could she be? Potassium on water, our passionate desire
changed us for the better."
                    Jude pondered. "A holy sadhu will grieve
for Krishna, Arjuna and the world by smearing ashes on his head;
the ashes of desire; acceptance is the sleeper's, not the lover's bed."

She left by train from a dipped platform. My lovers always do,
and yet before she went she gave me that long last
kiss; the kiss that seals.
                    The rest's mundane. I bought a vindaloo
and took me to the cut, the brackish sad canal that runs past
Old King Street and neath a bridge on Windmill Lane. There
I sat me down and wept.
                    Finished. My world was in despair.
What had I left? Some memories of things past we'd come to share,
some swan's down and ten letters, not even one lock of her hair.

I had a brown half Anna, a lover's corny joke—'Two halves will make
a whole'. We'd bought it at the Goose Fair, Nottingham. 'Half a buck,'
I'd said, "for you Imperatrix—My Empress.' Laiking was over, my say
in her life finished, I knew that I must now throw it forth. My luck
would not run out. It never does.
                    Into the Soar I threw that Hindu dollar.

When I looked up beside me stood a man with an insect on his collar."

"A ladybird," said Jude?
       "A Ladybird for sure making its humble way
across the Chinese laundered winged collar he habitually wore
to make himself distinctive.
       Why did we choose it. Some say
we knew of *Penguin* and their Antarctic cache. I'm sure
considerations of that kind have resonance and primal force.
In publishing images of birds or animals have validity.
Red and black, the Fascist colours also sells, though, of course,
money is always made when chance and need lie in close proximity".

He said, 'I want a new designer duck.' That's what he said,
'You seem as if despair has got to you and pulled you low.
Before you embrace your death give me a slick idea. I've read
swans sing before they die. I need a logo for I wish to show
my publishing exists and flourishes.
       When you've nothing left to lose
you risk all on the obvious."
       "Speak openly," he said, "you choose?"

"I'd choose a Ladybird,"
       I said. It now was crawling on his head
along lank greasy hair towards Nirvana. It's history? In an earlier life
it was a lotus flower which was transmogrified into a sadhu, who, instead
of standing with his sleek head in the sand in clear contempt of strife
and pain, lowered himself. That done he looked around
and made the business Retail. His most obvious feature
was the navel that he contemplated.
       The man before me stamped the ground
and smote his forehead with his hand; that way he killed the tiny creature.

He killed the Ladybird, but unlike mariners, he was not smote, rather
he grew elated. 'By shots, you're good,' he said. 'Well bugger me
I've paided consultants but it's you who fast delivered. I gather
that youre unemployed. No more you're not. Name the fee,
then name your name?"
       "What is my name?" I know it seems absurd.
I answered the best way I could. "I am Wynkyn of the Worde"

That is a powerful alias, a name to make a printer's rafters ring.
Wynkyn came from Alsace and set up shop in distant Herts.
Although he carved neat moving type, proof–reading was his thing.
He also knew of upper case and lower case. A man of many parts
was Wynkyn. *Publisher* it said upon his sign; knight on a horse,
his logo. Amongst his titles was *The Little Geste of Robin Hood*,
the book that said the hero lived in Nottingham. Of course
not all agree. I believe he lived in Pont or Cas, but then I would.

Best choose an alias in one great lightning flash
then hold to it through thick and thin, and don't discard it
lightly. Wynkyn de Worde, the name, had liveliness, had dash
and much beside that's why I stuck with it. I had the ready wit
and could design. I'd hype but not the ready money.
                                                      He seemed
to read my thoughts, said, 'Here's a Newton note.'
                                                      I'd dreamed

of miracles and now one held me arms length in his arms.

I was in work and had, or so I thought, a job for life.
I also had a mortgage and a spaniel. When false alarms
arose, rode into them. The elegant, ivory handled knife
that cuts through *Ivel Butter* cut into my work–a–day days
and thence divided all to pats. I would arise at eight, at nine
be at my table sharpening; luncheon, one to three. I'd go to plays
each second Tuesday in the month, there drink the choicest wine.

Each printer is a slave to orders. Apprentices ensure the furniture that
stacks around flat beds is made of hard woods or an alloy you can fettle
if needs you must. They understand the language of the letter press, what
font is stylish and how to print a bill.
                                         If you know this then settle
promptly, if not, prepare you'll find small justification in an imposition.
When all the stock is inked think upon Humanitas and our condition.

Mann managed by expletive. Said 'Fuck off,' 'Bollocks' and 'You Prick,' little
else yet each one got the drift. When extra pleased he'd say 'You Silly Sod'
or 'Wonder Twat'; when angry 'Bloody Fool' and 'Silly Bastard'. Jot and tittle
politness passed him by. Foreigners, especially Indians, thought this conduct odd,
they managed through the network of the family. I was not shocked for I had
cursing uncles just like him, men who had few words, aunties on the game,
who would for ready cash whisper into phones strange oaths of love.

My dad
was born a Castleford Pratt. Yet for myself I'll never own the name.

(Although of ancient origin it is a family name that few would have by choice
for when its said naturalness declines; folk give at best an inward smirk,
at worse they state with emphasis and sometimes seem to stress the over nice
gap which goes before it and a former word. Families of Pratts would work
themselves into a lather listening for their name and then that breathing space).

We bought the printing sheds on Central Road. I came to love the place.

We settled in and that way our publishing ran on. Just like two cherries
on a single stalk that was the boss and me. Friendship was defined
by us for he lacked woman's love.

His wife had several sherries
(*Bristol, Crofts, Tesco Old Peculiar*) under the sink and under the crinolined
lady in the lavy room, the place where goodly matrons kept the spare
Andrex, she had a place for hiding booze. Theirs was an arguing household,
a total slatten always in pyjamas she had never heard of share and share
alike.

But back to publishing.

Why did Ladybird succeed? Easy. We sold
what folk in a suburb's streets desired; a vision of lawns and well
trimmed laurel bushes, hardy annuals, babies in gros and milkmen who tried
to satisfy; such cream. No burglaries. The Neighbours In From Hell
did not live in semis on their avenue. Paint was mint fresh, no one died
or threw a wobbly. There were no drunks; an image of a family life defined
by two small children; cosy, nice and comforting, one–up, refined.

Refined but not refined with antique furnishings, refined in such a way it was
obtainable; especially if you worked weekends. We piped, the workers
whistled. (Run Rover Run). Tea on the patio, no one obese. and so, because
all seemed in easy reach, they took the bait. We rationalised. Any shirkers
went to the Coalville pit, (Down Rover Down) What fools.

Our Ladybirds were learning manuals; those and bank loans. Folk left
the backs for Garden Lea and Fine Fairview. In built–in cupboards useful tools
lay swoddled down in bubble wrap, for screws were rare. The woof and weft
of shoddy cloth was overseen by overseers, the purl and plain of knitted socks
became our history. A winner we began to go upmarket. *Hand Tooled Creame
Deluxe* at 50 gram, the standard paper. Look in the FT Index you'll see our stocks
fast rose. Rejoice, Rejoice. (Bark Rover Bark). No *Uz and Them*
times those. We were One Nation under God and Gotcha.

All went well

for a decade and then the orders slumped.

(Sell Janet Sell)

In summer 97 decline set in (Janet's Failing, Falling Fast) I tried
to keep abreast but couldn't. Although I read the manuals how can a man
whose notion of design is scalpeling compare with men who plied
the Apple Mac® and Windows 95®. I looked inward and saw the span
of years I could expect begin to dip away. I thought, "Time to move on,"
but couldn't for I saw he needed me. We'd seen all sorts, ours was a true
Platonic friendship. He was the ying and I his yang. He said, 'Life is a con.
I once was poor and then we met. By backing you with capital I quick grew
rich beyond the realms of aravice. But now I'm overdrawn, my alcoholic
wife just raves and does a Mrs Rochester. I take her pills, have hid
the brandy and the brandy snaps and cream. Although a workaholic',
he clutched me to him, 'I'll never leave you, on my word'.

And then he did.

He met a Slady Miss, an Arts and Crafty girl, he called his niece,
and ran with her. She ran for all his worth. They made for Greece.

All roads lead to Rhodes and not to Rome, for there art
is a clear eclectic. Afro, German, Yankee–doodle, the art of mad folk
(real outsiders those), elephant–headed Ganesa, (in part
an Aryan, in part pure Science fiction) merges; the volk
art of the Jugendstil mixes in with robust Jubilee Line graffiti.
Beech planking from Rietvelds bungalow recycled here as Gerrit's chair
Never Fascist, all's just untidy. An Ibro fetish and a 'sgraffitti
Bull–Ring bowl by P. Picasso sits next to G. Stein and makes a pair..

Ancient Rome was not the Rome of Mr Minichiello (hands
and heart both very big) or of his boy, but the Rome
of Commodus—Caligula, bloody and sinister, where bands
of debauchees flocked to Solidarium. *There Is No Place Like Home*
was not their song. In Rhodes the East meets West and North the South
through longitude. Art is the Colossus at Rhodes's harbour mouth.

They had no time for me, for Wynkyn of the Worde. Enraptured
in each other's arms they slept the Grecian morning through
in a siesta, only waking up to read a pillow book. Captured
by Dan Cupid, though she was twenty and he was sixty–two,
they made the welkin ring.
                    One day depressed I picked my rucksack
up and bought a one way ticket. I'd Whittington down to Town
and leave the lanes of Loughborough and the Quorn. I'd back
my hunch and travel on. Though bashed about a bit I was not down.

The day I chose to travel was, or so it soon turned out,
the day that Dodi and Diana died.
                    (A sad date that, for sure,
they hit the thirteenth pillar – three dead and one the driver.) Why bang about
and sing the *My Way* song when all is out of canter, why sing when lives as pure
as theirs are lost in just one minute?
                    Life is a game of pitch and toss
with no clear rules, is little more than action. Theirs, *The Nation's Loss*.)

Before my train departs I must explain.
Space time and every alias
that you ever used or dreamed about, rests not on reason but on chance.
The Laws of Averages and *The Mean of Possibility* when in a looking glass
are reversed, therefore Lord Krishna in the Chariot and Siva's Cosmic dance
amount to truth for they are in the narratives of Gods, the rest is never true.
How can it be when we are all unique and all is back to front or upside down.
Retinal images tumble to salute Australia, the brain's a mystery, the skew
is spiralling DNA.
And yet there's hope. Not every English wights a clown.

In the fifth carriage of the Virgin train a buffet carrying sachets of *Suppa White
Granulated Sugar* in a plastic dish. Between the stirrers and that dish,
jammed in a visiting card which read in Bold Helvetica, Nick Cooper–Kite
— Cardboard Engineer. I took the Astrolux card and made a wish.
'Forgive me all my tresspasses'—and then in vain I filched his name.
If Standard Carriage folk like me had next to nought they'd do the same."

I reached St Pancras as the clock struck one and since I carried next
to nought I wandered to Great Russell Street, avoided traffic in the Strand
and bridged the Thames at Southwark. Literature now my sub–text.
Oh yes I knew this place; its streets were paved with gold. I had not planned
this route but here I was, back–packing into history. The medieval poet Gower
lies buried in St Saviour's blackened Church, here Chaucer left the Tabard
Inn en–route to Beckett's tomb. Past here, down to the Bloody Tower,
they rowed young Surrey to the Traitors' Gate, and death. Wyatt, hard
on his heels, another poet. Shakespeare owned a property on Bankside.
Here stood the bear pits and the *Globe*, also the stews where mackerel men
sold whores. Burbage played Hamlet with a crowd which couldn't quite decide
if *All Was Well* or life a tragedy. Here Kemp danced on and Afra Behn
played parts, here Fletcher lies entombed. Inspired I couldn't fail to win.
I tracked past Rotherhithe to Deptford Town and to the Mermaid Inn.

The Mermaid Inn, I knew that place. That's where Kit Marlowe died
surrounded by his drunken mates. He'd pissed himself; stabbed through the eye
because he would not pay his way. Marlowe, the atheist who tried
to sell his soul for fame. *Faustus, Malta's Jew, Tamber The Lame*—spy,
poet, playright—'a great reckoning in a little room.'
                                        Thinking of stinking fish
and ripe young breasts, I crossed the brig of Ravensbourne. With gold comb
in her hair and in her hand a bevelled mirror, a mermaid; old dying sailors wish
to hear her song. "The Thames," I thought, "is deadly, is another tomb."

There were two ladies sitting on the Mitre steps, I showed
them courtesy and sat with them. Their bed became my bed, a bed
of stone beneath a mangy blanket. Theirs was a world slowed
to the grace of the last waltz. I liked them instantly therefore instead
of moving on I stayed. Admired by them I listened to suggestions.

That roughly is my story up to now. Please have you any questions?"

"How come," said Jude, "that Mrs Mills has said she saw you
a—cutting cardboard in the Mall on Diana's wedding day and yet you said
you went to London only on the day that Dodi died. Both can't be true."

He paused and smiled then gave his knowing look. "You're wed
to Linear Time, I dodge about, for one dense crowd is very like
another, the second carried wreaths enhanced by cellophane,
the first had flags and fancy hats; all had travelled far, some by hitch hike
others came by train; the rich had retinues and landed close by aeroplane.
I travelled down a wormhole."
                                "I did that very thing but two hours
since," said Jude. She grew excited straining to explain. "It's gross
but Mega—Gee exciting. I'll give you here a parallel. At Alton Towers
there is a ride that cogs you up by rack and pinion rail until you look across
the plains of Cheshire, then drops you so your mind spins with acceleration.
Ultra Wow!"
                Spare time for fantasy, know that and we will be a healthy nation.

Let's move along the bus.
                    "I see there on the Mitre steps a basket full
of wire and paper scraps, a bucket full of scissors made in far
Taiwain and purchased bulk. That means even the pull
of Art extends to steps where drolleries wait the dawn. You're on a par
with artists everywhere, under–valued so you're underpaid. You dream
yet know the best work's done when in a company of sundry folk. That said
you're also on your own and there's the paradox. You're by yourself yet in a team.

I am industrious you see I'm working here on what I now call Project Zed.
a book on London life and venal sin. Though up to now it lacks a name
it borrows from the *Book of Lady Di*, also from books I made for Ladybird,
the musings of the Persian Magi and the Hindu *Gita*. Yet still I cannot claim
it is unique, for no book is, and yet I'll say it is important, though not the Word
of any God, for it is harmless. In every way this is a very special book."

Jude: "Say more. There's bottle washers everywhere but you're a cook."

"The pop–up bouncy castles in my book are quite spectacular. One
will inflate and stand erect. It's based on London's famous Tower.
There also is a Traitor's Gate with a portcullis. The stone
is Dulux Grey, the windows are matt black. Upon the hour
a sign appears *Watch Amazed The Tragic Death Of Anne Boleyn
— Decapitation With A Sword.*"
                    Jude read the sign and said,
"I learn from signs so am untouched. Adultery is a heinous sin
but can't compare with chopping off some poor queen's head."

More sins are listed on a one inch Velcro strip
which runs along the top. Jude reads them out aloud
and sighs. Few sins excite her for she's young, yet sins can trip
you up if you're not on your guard or very proud.

"The wages of sin—or so the Bible says—are Death,"
Jude sighed. "Adulterous Anne's twopenneth."
                                        "Underneath

five other sins are cited. Stealing from the poor house
box in Greenwich Church to buy a scratch card,
sleeping in a doorway in the Strand, using a louse
ridden blanket, borrowing lingerie from a sin bin yard
and wearing it new washed, possessing a machete or a knife
which won't cut butter but speaking oft of anarchy
and doubting primogeniture, sleeping with the foreman's wife
when he's on afternoons—a heinous sin for sure; for hierarchy
always is an issue with the powerful and its over easy to mix
beyond your class and cause confusion."

                                   Jude: "Trivial enough
these sins seem when I read them out aloud, hardly sins at all. Fix
them in aspic and the gut reactions which I get don't call my bluff
or move me till my bowels get liquidised. Hell is burning coal
clean. So it and godliness combine well upon the whole."

Canto Nine

The Old Observatory

As Time and Tide passeth away
so doth the Life of man decay.
Since it's redeemeth at no cost
Bestow it well and Let no hour be lost.
Lines engraved on a clock at Townley Hall

Jude and Karen meet Mandy, they were all at school together. They walk to the Observatory. After looking through a telescope she decides to go and look at the Dome from close up.

Jude left them on the Mitre Steps and crossed the road
into a street of shops which specialised in selling sailors' knots,
Boxing–The–Compass, Nelson's death mask, telescopes. Spode
Ware showing a rescue by Grace Darling, maps with brown spots—
the sort you can remove by using all your liquor ration. (A cure
for every ill is rum but do not dab too hard.) That said, there is a fashion
for preserving foxing and distressing.

Jude: "A mariners' street for sure."

The wind is Westerly. The afternoon is making for the perfect night
when heaven's near. The one which follows when you've rushed around
and need to settle in a comfy chair and kip.

A small electric light

has come on in the park and so she makes towards it. A rhythmic sound
draws her to Time's trysting place. "I think of Kingdoms yet to come"
says Jude, "the rhythm I hear beating on and on is like a tabla drum.

Yon drum is like my pulse rate. Even in dreamland it is always there.
It tells me that I'm quick and am not dead but hints that it could stop
most any time. Then all is silence. It has a quality we share
with creatures who've warm blood."

Beside the iron gates a tiny shop,

a mere five metres square, it's painted council green, steel shutters
have been raised. The light, still on, illuminates its owner.

"It's late,"

she speaks confidences to a customer. "I'm fair fed up. My gutters
have come loose."

Standing by dunking biscuits; Karen Micklethwaite.

"Jude love, meet Mandy." The round lass sitting on a stack
of stacking chairs does not smile: Karen: "Mandy always wins."
Jude seeks her out inside her filofax.

"Born at the back

of our Bill's mothers up in Gladstone Street, called Mandykins
by mates, though straight Amanda Pet's her Sunday
name. Moved down to London saying she'd not stay."

Jude thinks: "She's put on weight yet I'd know her anywhere
for she was in my set for Maths and English both,— but chose
to wander off before her GCEs were passed. We thought her
free but thankless. 'A sullen bitch,' said some but those
who'd camped with her on Ingleborough, seen her little legs
scarce touch the scree when dangling over Gaping Ghyll,
will recognise her other side. To say she is all excellence begs
many questions. Yet more than most she lives to drink her fill."

"Is this place yours?" says Jude.
                       Mandy: "I have it on a mortgage
from the Halifax, but I am not alone in that, for most folk do;
few own their assets. My shares are listed on the YP Business Page
most days and that is why I got the *Guardian* hype which makes folks go
to great lengths just to eat at *Mandy's Place*. From far and wide
they come wishing to sup. Look through the menu seeking to decide,

and when they come I satisfy and pleasure them. The loving cup
gets passed around with style. A character trait I share
with gourmet Irving and with Mandelson. Like me they sup
upon the very best that's found in any lock–up kiosk anywhere.
It's Egon Ronay right. I keep my *Snickers* in the fridge
and bring them forth clap cold. My *Pepsi* lies on blocks of ice,
my milk comes fresh Spode.
                       I am the cantilever bridge
between the working and the chattering class, like the *Nice
Biscuit* I fit anywhere. I'm found at Numero Ten and Highgrove,
dealing sweetie–pies to diplomats and Smarties. I'm on
inner circuit for I'm where its at. I'll tell you this much, Karen love,
get in with me and you'll go far. In Newest Labour terms I'm One
Of Us. I'm singled out for space in *Marie Claire* and in *Hello*
as someone you should watch. I'm in your face for I'm on show.

And since they've built down by the Thames that great erection
folk flood down here to gawp. The numbers have increased
a hundred fold and will get worse come Jubilee. A selection
of lines will go through Greenwich Town; Wonders have never ceased
through out the time I've run this caf. But this I'll say,
since Mr Fayed's bought the site things have looked
up for he's a gentleman of vision. At work and play
he shows all courtesy, honouring all. The cooks who've cooked
his broth across the years, though many, are all good. Yet death
has hit him hard. Dodi was his first born and so the thrust
of grieving was no joke. But he fought back.
                              Jude: "When breath
comes in short pants, when slobbering and the sobbings done we all must
build constructively."
                Mandy: "You see that's not a Pleasure Dome,
a trivial place, but one of family values. Yon, it's said, is Dodi's Tomb."

Keith, Karen's first born, here looked up and seemed
to want to speak but Mandy cut him short.
                                "Two years
at least I've waited in this hut for you. I dreamed
that you'd come here and bail me out. Three Musketeers
they called us when we rushed around the infants' school
bawling, colt trotting, hair a–flare, arms linked behind our
backs, girls in harness, happy each with each.
                                More fool
I to leave the climes I knew—Cas streets—to gad about. My hour
has come. It's time to move. Though famed as *Mandy's Place*
the business that is here is on the rocks. It is back–home–
time here for me. I'll rover back to Featherstone, buy a grace
and favour shop in its Main Street. Folk shouldn't drink standing alone
at counters. Elegance demands a cup and saucer venue. A Yorkshire brew
is better than all the tea in China or that arriving daily from Typhoo".

"You'll give it up," said Jude, "and live on Station Lane?"
"Too right I will—London isn't all that it's cracked up to be.
Mandy's Place this cafe's famous far and wide, but it's a pain
to work here morning, noon and night. Get a philosophy."

Jude: "You think you *am* because you *are*. René Descartes
said that. Don't be half soaked, but fully soak yourself until
life's natural oils seeps in at every pore. Be like the Sagittarian—part
man, part horse—although you'll fire straight arrows do not kill
the hen who lays the golden eggs."
        "Mixed metaphors," thinks Karen,
"invade a maiden's mind if she lives long beyond the sticks.
In Greenwich Town or Islington the diet's over rich."
        But then
it usually is if all you have is hype and through glossies get your kicks.

"When we have dunked *Nice Biscuits* we will climb the distant hill
to the Observatory, look at Harrison's Clocks; Haitch One to Three, fill

our time with Time. That done we'll see the Dome."
        "That seems
a good idea. We are not sheep and goats, can't say who shall
and who shall not go visiting: sweepers–up have dreams".

"But come inside. I'll pull the shutters down so we can kal
till supper time and then some more. I'll shut up shop,
will make a brew, unlatch the coupling of my bra, let all
fall forward, lounge as comfy cat, or regular milk sop.
I pour us all a gin and tiny tee, set up to have a ball.
Take down some *After Eights* for starters.
        A mere five
metres long the shop, but being small is beautiful and creates
an ambience that stimulates the soul."
        Jude: "She'll thrive
because she's not herself to blame but blames us all. She states
the obvious, but then she always did. Mandy never brooks delay."

"I'll root out *Doze–Time–Put–Me–Ups* if you would like to stay."

"It's nice of you to ask. You always were my sort of sweetypie
but we can't settle, the end is almost here. I cannot rest until
I've tested if tomorrow never comes. I can't accept. The *I Spy
Book Of Time* had yon upon its cover." She points on up to the hill
to the observatory. "We must go there."

Mandy sloughened, sheds a tear
or two. "I've offered all I've got. I know it never is enough
but losers can't be picky." Fighting for control. "Take up your gear
and climb the hillock, in spirit I am with you, and if the going's tough
bite on these bars."

With this, from out the fridge she takes five
Snickers, looks Judith in the eye. "These are the sort we'd stack upon
the Tesco's shelves when all those years ago—dead or alive—
we nightly partied. We worked the tills. Jude begone;
you to your destiny, me to mine. You'll never look
on Mandykins again."

They do as they are told, they take their hook.

Since she has said, "Begone," they quickly go. Behind a crying
Mandy shuts up shop. She empties rubbish into plastic bags, breaks
up cartons, collects the cans which make all spick. Trying
not to weep, as she remembers Zion, snuffles, "Your coming awakes
in me a memory of things long gone which few can ever satisfy
on this side of the grave."

"You can't turn back the clock,"
that's what Jude's dad had said and now they went to try
to do just that. They climbed the hill seeking to unlock
the mysteries of Linear Time. "Why must we have our
yesterdays, *Instant Coffee* time but know tomorrow never
comes for Time romps on regardless. We have the power
to impose systems, be in control," Jude says, "Lifes like a fever,
do not feed it, just think on justice, feed the poor."

They reach a destination but find a well barred door.

The sun is setting on the West. Jude saw that now.
The West was flim–flab, boot–up, fashion, super–hype
and not much else it seemed. She wrinkled up her brow.
"All's lost."
                    It weren't. Although the door was shut Dave had a swipe
card. They were quickly in.
                    "I designed this plastic, but
a long time since." He then went on to tell her all he had
designed on from his Loughborough days. At *Pizza Hut*
the Cardinals' Hat that glows red in the night, *Mad
Harry's* logo—a man who bites upon a haddock fish,
beneath a chandelier close on Ilkley's Cow and Calf. The *Phil
Ate Steak* you get as pub grub everywhere. The *Death Wish*
ride at Alton's turreted Towers, *Tesco's Curiosity Till*,
the one that opens on command. *The Box For Good Intentions,*
from which you get five tenners, is one of my inventions."

The night watchman's now has gone to slumberland. His mattress
is a stack of brochures sculptured plainly by that
genius, the Man Who Can Sleep Anywhere. In the caress
of massive kip he sleeps. They tip toe to another door. What
seems a barrier isn't. "Sez Me," that is the personal phrase
that Dave will use to unlock this portal.
                                        They stand outside.
It's gloaming time and therefore all is well. A craze
of glittering ranges wide across the Northern sky; a wide
panorama is on view. Canary Wharf, a red light
on the top to draw King Kong if he should wander in
takes centre stage, flood lit St Paul. "Some sight,"
says Jude. The others nod assent. "I feel akin
with all who have a sense of presence."
                                        A fine
brass strip runs right across the yard; it's the Meridian Line.

Jude opens wide her legs and straddles it, one leg to
east, the other west, and looks to the North star. The scene
is hers. "I'm one with longitude," she says, "now I stand on true
zero. I feel my time has come and cleaves at me."

Below a pasture of lush green,
now dusky grey, as new night stretches Thames–wards. This sward
of grass runs to a boundary wall. She looks on Mandy's coffee shop
standing beside the gates inside a pool of light to the leeward.
Lovers move to it. "They're holding hands," Jude now. "They'll stop
and buy a plastic cup of *Instant*. Tenderly fill it to the brim
with milk and add three sugars smiling. Dusk is the key
of tender love."

Like Shylock's Jessica she says this to the stars.

The rim
of day is etching at the northern hills. She can see
the Queen's House so says unto herself, "This view has charm."

Feet firm, well set, stock still, Jude stretches out her left arm,

and then the right. Behind her, Karen's kids both do the same. They stand
astride the line.

Jude turns and smiles: "We're like the concertina men
folk tear out from the *Evening News*."

Karen: "Or else you are a band,
a trinity, based upon the perfect man Da Vinci drew when
searching for a human order. In rich red crayon he drew him
naked in a circle in a square."

"You're right" Jude knows the
image. When a girl she bought some stationery upon a whim
at *Smiths* in Ponte Market. Seated at home her dad had eyed it.

"I see,"
he said, "yon's now a logo. Such elegance. Once it was Da Vinci's pipe
dream of perfection. What a graceless world we're living in.
Artist's names for Ninja Turtles, and now there's this. All's hype
and flim flam. Think on this thought young Jude. There is a thin
red line that goes between the crowd of effers and good taste.
It's called decorum." He sighs his sigh. "Without it all must go to waste."

"Oh rare humanity" says Jude and laughs.
Karen has found
a telescope. She looks through it. Fixed to a stone base
it takes all in that lies due north.
"There is a darkened foreground
then lit–up rooms in Greenwich Hospital, beyond that empty space,
and then the Thames at night."
Jude: "Does the line go through the Dome?"
Karen: "Almost, but not quite; it is at least a shaving to the East."
"And through Canary Wharf?"
"The same, but West."
"Come
on," said Jude, "that's carelessness, poor planning. At least
our Yorkshire architects would have made a point when tendering."

Another voice. "Three years ago that was a brown field site of derelict
factories, lean–tos and working people's terraces. The rendering
of that history would interest you. Inhabitants long since, tricked
of inheritance, have wandered off to buy a flat inside a tower block
and seen their equity plummet, though they have shares and stock."

The voice that says these words comes from a man
who squats against the outer wall. He seems to be
at one with dusk itself, he's so ethereal. "There was no plan
to move them on except the market, then well beloved."
He
pauses and seems to sneer when talking. "Monetary theory
was the thing those days, such and think–tanks. State intervention
was the Devil's spawn when Maggie Ruled Okay. They did not query
if Lloyds' Names were charlatans, never asked their true intention."

Jude: "You are a pessimist for sure. And yet today the cynical
have qualities we all need as we face up to life and learn
a lot." She thought of The Three Graces of the Spring. "It's cyclical
is the dance so it will come around again. The art is just to turn.

Dear Misterman you've clearly wandered far and wide.
And so have we. I think I know you, can you be our guide?"

Ram smiled "With pleasure."
                    "Do I know you," out blurted Jude?
"I've seen you often when I've gadded forth upon the trains
and walked routes of this town. I hope this won't sound rude,
you sat a few seats back upon the Docklands. Because I hold the reins
life I spotted you. In the glazed tunnel you sat alone
and banged an Oxo box. Yours is a corner shop. I notice most things."

Before him was the very cloth of burnished gold, the one
on which his trinkets stood when she had seen him first. Gold rings
and ankle bangles from Samarkand, an Onyx box from far Tashkent
the sort that Tambur, who was lame, had used to keep his powder dry,
a Rolex watch from Tiffany's; also one pearl, lay there; heaven–sent
objects each and every one. Inheritance their origin, you'll never buy
the like of these; no sleight of hand, no complicated ploy
could conjure them. This treasure of Ram Bhajan was the real McCoy.

She chose a bracelet with a beryl clip and put it on her arm.
"A wise choice that for girls who wander. My name is Ram
and you are gentle Jude," the seer said.
                    "A charm
offensive this for sure," she thought. "*I think therefore I am*;
is known to such as he. He clearly is a major Hindu god
but who he is or where he goes I cannot quite be sure.
There are so many in that pantheon. Some benign, others odd
by any standards; some pray, others walk on fire, some cure
the poor and sick, others batter demons and small fry,
remove small warts who can't be charmed away
with amulets, thread needles through their backs and cry
in ecstacy even when times are good."
                    What could a smart girl say
yet not be dumbstruck.
                    He spoke his calling card,
                    "I also think because I am
Like you I'm positive. The peasants of the Punjab towns just call me Ram.

"Pleased to meet you Meister Ram," said Jude. "This is my mate.
We worked on the Tesco's tills a long time since and now
we've come this far we'll take some stopping. Karma and Fate
both grip us. Karen meet Ram. The boy's her son. He cannot show
emotion. His Sunday name is Keith. We met beside the Clipper Ship
at just gone noon. The girl who's playing over there, her daughter Kay.
Keith is the first born, she her youngest child; he's inward, she is a slip
of a girl, coarse, distracted, hair out of place, yet always has her say.
I do not know why they are here but I am here to speak my mind.
I've thought things through and speaking out is my prime function
in this busy life. I'm curious, needs must know. 'Seek and ye shall find'
the text was on my Granny's cottage wall and so I echo that injunction
everywhere. You see I need to know the meaning of the Trinity
found in yon cabinets: *Haitch One, Haitch Two, Haitch Three*."

Jude knows the new man's name and that he holds the place
that few gods hold. This Ram's an incarnation of the
God himself. Sensitive, strong, in tune with space
and time and all the mysteries they hold, he
is the messenger, the guide that Hindus need to take
them on their travels through ethereal worlds and up toward
the Ganga's source. "He'll more than do," says Jude, "no make
and mend god this but Vishnu reincarnate."

In Castleford,
where two rivers merge and where the broken boat rocks
on the weir, we sense the worth of such a one as he.
He comes as valued–added. Rare as handmade socks
in Loughborough, Ram Bhajan is welcome for he's the key
that can unlock the outside lavy door on a wild night.
Constant as a tabla beat heard made by one hand against pure light.

Karen's lad had followed her across the courtyard
and in the second room had seen the Astrolabe.
He knelt before it musing. At first he found it hard
to make it out and yet he persevered. Each decade
someone somewhere will read the words and be so moved
it changes them. Mohammed Khalben Hassan
made this eloquent device eight centuries since. It proved
you learn things from the stars but you should plan.

*The aim of this object is that something may be
made for us, for we know we will not live forever.*

Keith reads the words first silently and then aloud. Notice we
all do this when we are moved. He has authority. "Clever,"
he says, "he's linked his life through mathematics to the panoply
of universes. Muslims love the stars, they revel in astronomy."

The boy moves on. Is there emotion in his words?
Though rather flat Jude thinks there is. It's then
she speaks.
        "Someday he'll find his vocal chords
and sing the Music of the Spheres. Ptolemy taught that when
all seven heavens move, the sensitive can hear a high pitch
sound which some can imitate and so gain wisdom. He's Westward Ho
but Eastward bent this singular boy. He'll stitch the stitch
that holds the other nine and not look back. This one can show
us all a thing or two. He knows what's going off. He imitates
today but soon I know he'll show his pace, speak out his mind
and I will listen? I've watched him grow and that creates
a dialogue for he will hide then seek, seek and then he'll find.
That's when he'll sweep us all along as a new broom."

Thinking thus she walked along into another room.

Jude gazed upon the row of clocks that Harrison had made
in competition with the best there was. Jude: "He'd moved
from Foulby, not far from Pont and Cas, and here's displayed
his handicraft. Brussen *Harrison Haitch One* (Beloved
of the scientist Halley), then *Harrison Mark Two*. When I look
closely, though all looks brass, the cogs and all the crucial moving
parts are wood."
        Last year she'd found inside her poke the book
called *Longitude*. A tale of daring–do and progress. Hovering
between science and biography it suited Meister Blair's Third Age.
Designed to stow inside a pocket, close to the heart it was a mood
piece. Was Science there to entertain Art? She'd turned each page
in wonder.
    Unity of Time and Place
                    Harrison watching the pendulum flood
advance and then fall back Hullwards. A man meditating upon the motion
and the rising tides.
        "That wasn't hype or self promotion."

Small is beautiful.
        An Arab girl upon the Docklands train had had a Spice
Girls' watch which glowed in wonder and now inside the final case
sat something similar *Harrison Four*. Reduced to hand size it is precise
to a fragment of a minute, even today it is a wonder.
                  Small space
hold futures in a coiled spring and pledges them along a train of gears.
Three hands and yet the noise of one hand clapping is never heard
for here all's scientific, never mystical. This explains why no one fears
the balance wheel. There are three clocks, the greatest is the third.

Ram: "Yes things will go awry and cogs won't mesh if a screw's loose.
Best be precise we must have peace with Time. We need to know both latitude
and longitude, also the star systems. The Universe is always neutral. Abuse
of power upon this massive scale cannot corrupt. Each minute is a platitude
of Time and Space, and can be used to track the time it takes to take a coal
to Newcastle or shoddy cloth to Dewsbury, but not distances in a wormhole."

Jude: "What is a wormhole?" Ram explains, the boy looks on.
                                                    "No one
has time. I'm sure you've heard that said. What is really being
recognised is more than words convey. I'm not alone
when I say this. The panic to be *On Time* oft drives us. But seeing
that is not enough. Where Time's concerned much is delusion.
In every brain there are two clocks. One is a stop watch,
the other takes the Time Frame of a day. What brings confusion
into reckonings is mixing of two clocks which do not match.

Karen's boy piped in "A wormhole is the route my mediator and
my Prophet (Peace Upon Him) took up to the stars. He saw the
sea of mosques which steadily rose across the boundaries of sand
which still divides the Arab and the Jew. With Gabriel he went forth to see
the prophets of the Torah. At Mount Zion he found them orbed in light.
He rode on from Arabic Medina unto Jerusalem in just a single night.

His steed was Bur'raq. A winged wonder horse quite
like the piebald filly the Grecian Perseus rode to meet the jinn
Medusa. He travelled through a wormhole. Upon Meraj, the Night
of the Ascent, he rose through seven heavens, transcended sin
and looked on God; all this within the twinkling of an eye.
He travelled upward through a wormhole. The Qur'an
does not use that term and yet this happened. With certainty I
know the way my prophet travelled.
                                        You see, each man
is dust and it is made quite clear he will return to dust.
The One–God Allah, all seeing though remote, alone
in Paradise awaits us. We are obliged to put our trust
in him. Come say with me "Allah great God you're One"
He paused for breath then said, "La ilaha i allah."   .
(Mohammed, Prophet) "Wa Muhammadur rasul al–Lah"

Ram nodded in assent. He showed the reverential calm
and courtesy a Brahim shows when listening to another's
wisdom. A boy preaching in a sacred place did not alarm
him for he knew the precedents. "This boy has mother's
love, the sort of love the Virgin gave to Christ, real treasure,
the love that Yashodda gave to Krishna, yon a vast trove
of great affection; a love which goes beyond the Pleasure
Dome right to the heart of our humanity."

Ram spoke of love.

"It's strange to hear a boy speak in that way," said Jude.
"He speaks with great respect about religion. Where does
he get it from. In Castleford few know of Islam beyond crude
images of Mullah's beards and scimitars. But then in Cas we chose
to show great ignorance of the outside world. We never care.
Our lack of knowledge is as wide as is the River Aire

near Lock Lane weir."

(That is the weir on which a British Coal barge,
broken from its moorings balances upon a powerful fulcrum point
and rocks, so gently rocks, to that flood time.

"By and large
we do not choose our symbols. When times are out of joint —
and this age is — they choose themselves and have their way
with us, (testing, testing) until we fail to get the point or joke.
A preaching boy and balancing barge mean something. Let's say
that symbols always talk to us.

Example: My mother's dad had woke
up happily then simply disappeared. A nice man, Pop. He had gone
for a quiet walk, a "Put–the–tea–on–for–I'll–be–back–by–ten"
stroll along the river's northern bank. That day he was alone.
My Gran would usually go, but she was making parkin. When
he had left her this last time she'd tucked his scarf in. "Don't stand
about, it's cold."

"Don't fuss," he said, "I'm champion. This weather's grand."

His last words: "The weather's grand." Later someone had seen
him walking riverwards. A woman with a pram thought him the man
that stood and watched the rocking of the boat. "He had been
there a good half hour," she said, "timing it."

Ram to Jude: "Did he plan
to die?"

"I doubt it. There one second, gone the next.
Timing sometimes is compulsive. All they found, one telling denture,
a complicated piece of bridge work."

"Coroners verdict?"

"The final text—
suicide just discounted—his was Death By Misadventure."

"Thinking of suicide is an act of balance," said Karen now, "*To be
or not to be*, six words that will repeat and rock us all to sleep.
Before the undertaking man closes our eyes we're said to see
our life pass by."

Jude: "Time and Wormholes seem everywhere. We keep
to constant images. We say, "His tickers stopped, he is clearly food for
worms. Was the boat on the Aire weir rocking towards a distant shore?"

Unanswered questions start new conversation. "Do numbers ranked below
the zero point in mathematics belong to some exceptional, fabulous jinn.
Half multiplied by half becomes a quarter."

Karen lit the fuse. Show
logic to a thinking child and then stand back. They focus in
and soon there's such explosions they can't cope. E.g; the sum
of nought times ten is simply nought. Child think this through,
and see that factors multiplied by stars still stay at zero. We come
no nearer to the truth by simply measuring. At least that much is true.

Jude: "Advanced computers can't calculate an end to pi.
They reached two billion points a few months back
and stopped for lack of finance. Yet men'll drive on. The sky
is not a limit where the points of pi are paramount. To lack
precision data on the relationship of radius to circumference
creates poor linkage. Let's have a mission statement and a conference."

"But not on pi," said Ram. "There's matter much more pressing
than that recurring nightmare pi. Its decimal points go
on forever, it's like the stars. You're always second guessing
where a pi's concerned. Why call in experts who will seek to show
far finer ratios."

           Hearing this Jude perked. "Let's talk of leisure
and how fashion, hype, drugs, sex and rock–un–rock are quantified
within the good life. Let's numerate Charles Darwin's *Pleasure
Principle*: "How many orgasms must you have before you're satisfied?"

Ram smiles and muses "The trouble with a girl like Jude is that
she will half hear a word then stick with it through
thick and thin. She reads her *Marie Claire* and pat
all is revealed. Organisms? No, orgasms are the *Uhu glue*
which binds the glossies. Darwin just the founding clerk
of our survival. It's he who said "If we are to survive we'll work."

Hunter gatherers worked a two hour shift each day and then
lay back and looked up to the Northern Star seeking a plan
projecting lines back to the Plough with trigonometry.
                                (When
measuring space through time count every pulse.)
                                       Later in a caravan
making for Makka the Prophet, Mohammed (Peace Be Upon His Name)
saw new points of light in the Constellation of Sagittarius, a man
–cum–horse firing arrows, but opted for the Moon. He came
and preached a sermon to the Makka men; said "Those who plan
to follow me and my ways will know the certainty of leaving nought
to chance. I looked at star charts and there saw that you divide
the day by prayer times, made laws so that adulterers caught
in the climax of a kiss are stoned to death, saw we must provide
for the needy, give charity to the blind, strength to the far sighted.
Better than the Bible, in the Glorious Qur'an, all colours are united."

Canto Ten
The Pleasure Dome

In Xanadu did Kubla Khan
A stately Pleasure Dome decree
Where Alph, the sacred river, ran
Through cavern measureless to man
Down to a sunless sea.

Samuel Taylor Coleridge.

In which they see the inside of the Dome, meet a poet and get a lot of explanations, alliances are made, there are transformations but not everything ends happily ever after.

"The small lamp over there is the first star, the one that Home
Alone a small child wishes on. This is a day when all is for the best,"
said Jude, "I know that now."
                              In the shadows a *Wittner Metronome*
beats out a steady rhythm; it is Adagio.
                                          I've passed some test
by coming here but what that test can be, I cannot say.
I think I've got somewhere, learnt many things. *Mandy's Place*
was an illusion, my slumberland mattress. If I delay
too long I also know that I could fail so I'll move on. A head case
from the Northern shires, that's me, always wanting more
striving to emulate and tick another box. Mostly my curiosity
is a court card though sometimes it is like the monkey's paw
on which you make three wishes. A tincture of pomposity
and innocent virginity—the last the Achilles heel—
of any growing girl, have kept me in control and yet I feel,

I feel intensively that I'm the sort of girl who given half a chance
would sprint along beside a moving Virgin train if I was loved
and wandering forth upon some daring–do. Guinevere to Lance-
lot, Bonny unto Clyde; their risks and storms are mine. The gloved
hand (the mortgage) will never stay upon my bony shoulder.
I won't play safe. Life goes too quickly, you learn to count
to ten and then it's almost gone. Not very passionate, colder
fish by far than I have said as much. The Arabic Mount
Bur'raq is the horse perhaps I'll gallop on when I get older."

"Come fly with me," said Ram, "the small embroidery I've spread
has magic properties. It's genuine Persian. Okay some folk will con
the gullible. A student of Arabia I'm sure you've read
about the Caliph of Baghdad and how Aladdin rode upon
a magic carpet. Join me knowing that my square provides
a similar function."
                     Pessimistic Jude: "Life can contain far easier rides."

That said she stepped onto the unknown then cast
her eyes about. Karen and the kids next on stood
beside Ram Bhajam. Zarathustra climbed on last;
six people on a damask just two metres square.
                                                    Jude could
not help but laugh. "Beam me up Scotty." Ram did.
All is in the mind therefore the rocket boosted. The surprise
of being high above the Dome propelled them on.
                                                    Look, hid
inside each man's subconscious is the hope of Enterprise;
that Mr Spock, with Captain Kirk and the maiden Vinda Lou,
will guide imagination to a place where few have been before
an alien state, the place where daring–dos get done, where true
unto ourselves we recognise a mind field where all is hype. No core
of reason holds it in its place. We're over easy, up beyond cloud nine.
Mandy's Place, is just the metaphor for an exploding mine

field. It's abstract so you can call it what you will. Inspiration
that's a word that some will use though frankly I will not,
for art is never one part that and nine parts perspiration,
with so much sweat our little cotton socks would rot.
Jude: "Yon wen is like Gadhafi's tent and strikes a distant chord.
I hear explosions but know that we advance through increments,
through notes. What has this to do with folk from Castleford—
floating above the Greenwich Dome thinking about Gadhafi's tents
I am not sure. Karen a scientist of sorts, me a whip–wop who is trailing
clouds of glory picking up hints and crumbs of comfort, young Kay
and Keith – Karen's two – Zarathustra – Dave, why are all five sailing
on a square with a guru."
                                "This," says Ram, "is like a Mummers' Play
and Mandy's Place is just a metaphor of *Government open handed*."

This said, with a sucking French–kiss noise, the damask landed

Close up the Dome, though not as weak as is the *Angel of the North*
seen from a train approaching Tyne's–side, simply does
not work. It's big but it's not over big, definitely it's not worth
eight hundred million for its bigness. Why does New Labour choose
to rock the boat for such a bauble? Based on a popadom
that Ricky Rogers saw fast rising on a flattened fired–up stone
when he was wandering Saudi, somewhere near Rabat, it has aplomb
but not too much aplomb. I doubt its worth for such are prone
to hyped–up exaggeration.

      "Although it is real big it's not Grade
One Heritage for it's not civically trusted. Clearly it has cost a bomb
has that," said Zarathustra. "I know a bit about the building trade.
I've carried in my youth the heavy hod and slaved inside that tomb
the Lump. Being a brickie taught me about the risers and courses
of concrete, wolf whistling girls and how to accumulate on horses."

Jude: "But what is on the inside? What joys are there to tempt
a family down from Heptonstall or from the Midlandshires,
from Ashby De La Zouch or Quorn? Commoners they're not exempt
from sense, no more from feelings, it's just that their desires
have budgets. What is the price?"

      "It's said, a Faraday,
all twenty pounds, is what each person pays as entrance fee;
a family forty–five.

     Jude : "I'll buy that puppy dog. If it's the *Worker's Play
Time Of All Time* I'll go. Come tell me about the wonders I will see."

"All's rumour," Zarathustra now. "This much we know, the food
is by McDonalds and that you do not grow a mite depressed
because they scent us all with *Joie–de–vivre*. The Great and Good
who know the detail say that the poor are bound to be impressed.

And in an aerial floor–show, flying through the air with ease,
ten spangled daring doers, high fliers trained on the trapeze."

Karen glances up in recognition, is bemused, but does not speak.
Is this her missing man? Is Zarathustra Dave, her ex,
the man who'd wandered off to get a Giro? Silent, weak
about the knees, she listens carefully. Earlier joys; sex,
drugs and rock–un–roll, those heavy staples that had ruled
and pinned their life when they'd first met, have drained away
to memory. (Memory's a must in life.) Yet never fooled
by superficial change she does not speak. Rapid decay
is natural in young love and yet it can be soonest mended
if you in later life, wear Scarlet's frock and, "Frankly do
not give a damn my dear".
                              Dave and Karen; their love had ended
when he had banged her door. A rocking boat and they the crew.
All was intense and purile An effer he, she then a silly cow.
Now she, a scientist; he a flash designer. Yes she could love him now.

She listens to his voice and though the voice has changed
she'd know it anywhere. It is the voice that whispered in her ear
and told her that the earth had moved and re–arranged
her clothes. Once coupling had held them close together, also the gear
that lovers buy from *Private Shops*: aphrodisiacs,
nipple clamps, see–through nighties; (gear from the waste
of sex that you find there), pillow books, basques, packs
of ribbed condoms in translucent green with minty taste.

This was the man who'd loved and left, so would
she risk all on one last, one loving, chance? Too right
she would. She smiled.
                              You might well ask how could
she? Come on know the world, see clearly, that as night
approachs we must learn to read the astrolabe, try
like Mohammed Hassan to face your future knowing you will die.

And then he smiles, but not the toothy smile
that he had smiled when but a lad, the smile that
said, "Well thanks for that I've come. My mile
was run in just four minutes and like the cat
that's on the mat, I've had the cream and now I'd best
be off. It's not the bam bam bam so Thank–you–mam;
the goofy smile of satisfaction. "Have a quiet rest
then to the same tomorrow," Then the wide smile of the clam.

And how he smiles.
                    The long lost man is finally found
they've moved to something new. A quiet understanding
couples these two together. but then they've common ground,
two kids and taxi to The Knowledge. This makes their landing
soft. There are no sanctions, there's just the freedom to roam.

And since the end is almost nigh, all six approach the Dome.

This is a Pleasure Dome times ten, or so it's said
on all the adverts Jude has read or heard about.
Yet how it plans to pleasure her she isn't clear. She'd read
it was the ultimate in sensual perception and yet without
a doubt it is a Wen that's hung in space with steel cable.

In the forecourt, upon a hardboard folding pasting table,
a mug of sharpened poet's regular pencils.
                              (A poet must be able
to write at length on what is next to naught and yet be malleable
of diction, parade his words with skill.)
                              Other tools; squares of card
to write upon. (*Astrolux* is the ideal for it reflects light on its nether side.
The other side absorbs it. Best know that when the rhyming's hard
you need light for enlightenment). A poet must not hide
his genius beneath a bushel but deliver forth, must thrust
his stanzas head first at the waiting world. Yes, scissors are a must.

The cord from the placenta must be severed that's why, surprised
by their creation, poets often talk of blood. Their word–hoard
is a rhyming dictionary of horror, and seminal fluids; disguised,
poets speak in metaphors.
                          "Jude: Is poetry the draught board
of the soul but not so black/white logical. Some verse comes free
and forms itself in ragged lines devoid of rhyme or robust reason.
More pity that," she thinks "for hard work, plus a rhyme, is key
to progress. Poetic melancholia, that mellow fruit is out of season."

Judes had enough of poets; they hoop–la her then romp
around as if she was puppy dog. She knows the sort. Frustrated life
has passed them by that's why they will invent unruly girls. Pomp
and pomposity rule their lives. Not hers. A fork and sharpened knife–
man's what she wants, not poet tasters. Someone with a wage packet
that he will open only in her presence, one with a tax bracket.

Behind the table sprawls this neat young man.
Emblazoned on his chest in painted heraldry,
the logo: Lies Are Us. Keats–like, he sits to plan
his strategy. Dome plc, have paid the poet's licence fee
to bring him down from Huddersfield and set
him here awaiting custom. He's paid to see
the magic of the place and scribble forth. He'll get
what he deserves; for he's deserving. "Oh to be
in–something–now" comes thrusting to his mind
as Jude walks up.
                   "If I was you and you were me,"
she says, "you'd get a proper job and seek to find
the truth through honest labour. Hard work's the key
to the grand life — not poetry." She's blunt. "I'd run a mile
if I'd a job like yours, it's too laid back."
                                        "Sit here a while."

She sits.
"Tell me about your life. Its ups and downs.
and why you've wandered up from Castleford wishing to share
this celebration."
                    He's moved from listening mode. "Your towns
might be five Wakefield towns for I can hear the River Aire
that rises from beneath God's armchair, Malham Cove,
trickling through each syllable you utter. You speak
my Kirklees tongue with variants; yet know that *love*
will ends all phrases, not to shed a clout *while* Easter week
is out. You *laik* with language yet your *a* is hard, so it falls short.
When taking *baths* in *castles* you pay *cash*. The craw, craw, craw
of Ted Hughes' *Crow* is ever present, so when you speak; taught
at that grandsire's knee, you use short *a* s. You're raw,
direct.
        His arrow's in her heart.
                                    Jude: "I love to hear you rabbit
on, it is dale water flushing in a gill. Most have lost that habit."

Weak about the knees and in behaviour not really quite correct
Jude listens and then questions him. "Would you say that love
is lower case, in fact a sort of punctuation, just like my dialect?
Love's used a lot where I come from. Heavens above
we're always saying *love* but never really meaning it.
                                                    "I suspect
you're very wrong and yet repetition of a word can mean a host
of things. Lack of imagination's one."
                                    He stands. Erect,
and powerful, he pronounces. "Marriage, not love, is post
and pillow in the homestead makes the perfect whole
of man and wife and two small kids. The spouse is not an has–bin,
but is a joy forever if you obey your nuptial vows. Mutual Soul
Music, like the Music of the Spheres, gets well below the skin
and swims along the blood stream making for the heart, nor is it as stale
as *love* in a Yorkshire phrase. Please tell me all your tale."

Jude tells her story. The poet from Kirklees listens with intensity.
Most real poets can do this. They recognise they've come to see
the light thats at the tunnel end by listening; the propensity
to be involved is a real art.
                              "This poem that I'm in quite worries me,"
says Jude. "Some bits are fine and yet not all's tied up. The End
is almost nigh, we're almost finished, and yet some clues to what it's all
about are scatter cushioned. All's loosely stitched. *Make Do And Mend*
comes to my mind."

                              Poet: "When the men from Porlock come to call
they break the writer's concentration. *Domes of Pleasure*
float amid the Sacred River. Floated is a word you'll need
to understand, for floating is what poets really love. *The Treasure*
Trove Book Of English Verse I've read a hundred times. To read
a book like that encourages mind–racing. Yet some despise
all lyrical poetry see verse as deep emotion in disguise."

"Within that early verse (Verse Seven) there is a clue. That verse
contains the clue. Study it closely. (Amen, amen). The first word is the last
word in the Lordly Prayer the Christians use. Few curse
their life a death approach, most say *Amen*. Upon the mast
of that great clipper ship, *The Cutty Sark,* a cross has got created
by upright and cross beams. Symbolism, as you see, is everywhere.
In lighted tunnels great cars clip the lesser ones. The overstated
case, here called a *Nation's Loss,* is the common stock that we all share."

"Speak on — My ear is much enarmoured to thy note,"
says Jude unto the poet.
                              (A stolen line but its appropriate here.
Titania unto the Great Bard's Bottom, a line Jude's learned by rote.
She thinks about that Grecian woodland scene and sheds a tear.)

"The saddest love is that that's unrequited, that love can send
a maiden mad. Think on Ophelia. Let's sit together so the years can pass."

He's heard that sentiment before from nubile women, best bring its end
with crudity. "Shakespeare uses short *a* as in his *Dream* and makes a arse a ass."

Poet: "Best bring this to an end, for there are women who will lust
for men who have the poet's licence especially if they're young
and do not give a damn. It's pitiful really, not romantic. The trust
they put in poets is quite dangerous. Poets use folk. We've sung
about our histories long enough, sung tragedy in all the Seven Ages.
So: Away The Lads. The best declaim on life but write for Problem Pages."

Jude: "The end's a dog who pisses on the poor, therefore
Amen. *The Place*, a sale with cardboard boxes. *The Time* is now.
Theme of the piece: style versus philosophy. Fighters for
justice get pissed upon. It therefore is important that we show
some muscle for you cannot take it with you. Shout the odds out loud,
so altogether now," roars young Jude, "There are no pockets in a shroud."

Jude yet again: "Close to the opening there's a gimmer by a ship
in the dry dock. He focuses in upon the figurehead, a semi–naked lass
in a short shift who holds a horse's tail. Before the slip
in time and wormholes, before orators speaking of class–
war, before the feisty girls upon the train, before the God–
head Rama will reveal he's Vishnu, or Dodi goes in Seine
for love, the writer focuses upon the *Cutty Sark*, in this odd
poem it seems he's going somewhere, but then it's also plain
he doesn't travel.

"That man's the author, a clerk of sorts. He'll slip
into the tale as a conceit."

Jude changing tack, "You stress the space
between the words?"

"Also a conceit, a journeyman writer's ego–trip
always leads to strange wordscapes. The art is to place
yourself upon the cusp. The proofer always is quite keen
to place a pause between Canary and its Wharf but not between

the feisty maiden's *lip* and *stick*.
          "Why?"
                    "A mystery. Language grows
by increments, but why it should in truth, well no one knows.
That's why some points lie unresolved. Writers on life,
will ramble about a bit seeking the *Unities*. There is a theme
of sorts but inconsistency will bound about. Man and wife,
safe in their bed beneath one floral duvet, wandering dream
land, are not the stuff of epic verse. (Unless you feed them cheese
at bed time. Yet even then the nightmare's ridden far away
before they shower.) They've kipper–in–a–box consistency. Sleaze
has no part in their life. They do not think on worms or on decay
—but then they rarely stir; they fart a bit and in that way delay
arousal. The beat of the hum–drum drum indicates the route
they take. Ignore them, be romantic, live by increments. Play
simple games with words.
                    I know a story called Meghdoot,
it's set in Akbar's Court about the time when Shakespeare was alive
a tale of love by quiet increments and how two lovers thrive.

But I'll not tell it now for it is Ramadan. There's somethings best
saved up for Horlicks' time. Exotic tales like this have salt when read
out aloud by Auntie Edna as the sand man puts you to the test
and closes tired eyes. Yet please remember this, all have this need
for romance on a magic carpet, something no Arabian Night
nor Disneyland, nor Mills and Boon, can spoil.
Speaking rationally to romantics never comes out right.
So come on message, use myrrh not *Johnson's Baby Oil*.

When marking time just don't stand still but steal. Lit Crit
is always simmering so you must baste with adjectives any line
that isn't good enough. Develop appetites, so wit
can get you somewhere. Remember only Gadarene swine
troughed and so you must bring scholarship to the boil.
Where ignorance is bliss, cook using counter foil.

They've reached the trysting place and therefore there they
say a tiny prayer for Pasts and Futures. That done they enter
in the Dome.
                    Everything's mint fresh, all newly coined, decay
seems far away. A rose tinted neon light, still centre,
just says "Dodi"; reminding us he's dead, also the reason
for his insane passing o'er — (Ill luck that was for sure.)
They do not pause but go on in. His life was just a season
mellowed. The *Kumquat of John Keats* is not his cure.

They pay the entrance fee in Stephensons: "That's steep."
says Jude. "Why do they think the people of the North will come
to Greenwich Town without a subsidy of sorts.
                                            Please keep
the change" she says and puts six pennies in a jar. "A sum
like this accrues with special interest. One Millennium on
these coins will make a mint; thats how a fortune's won."

A massive circle and at the centre a white square: "The Tomb,"
says Jude and looks down at her shoes in studied reverence.

Of course it isn't. This is the Harrod's cenotaph. The Dome
never was the resting place of Dodi, in no sense
this a grave. It's true the half witted, in a word the crude
of spirit, say it is, but then they would, for they know
next to nought; that's why they sing the *My Way* song.
                                                    Jude
raises up her eyes and looks around. "It seems to glow
in expectation for it is user friendly therefore reacts
to each of my ten senses. Yet all's decorum, you do not laugh
nor laik about in here; for like a gallery space it impacts
on matter and on mind. In that marriage it is the better half
of something that's got divided.
                            "That's what a cenotaph should do.
It's like the ship, that cenotaph, they found at Sutton Hoo.

[131]

(Close to the Suffolk Strand there were three mounds upon a gentle rise.
The smaller ones were sacked by robbers long time since; the
larger one untouched in thirty nine when men with shovels came to prise
the turfs away as summer sun arose. By noon a negative, a mystery.
Although this seemed a grave of sorts there was no corpse. A keel
of lapping planks sat imprinted in receiving earth; echos of oak and rusted
nails were all a–jumble. By the stern, pots and treasure; and yet no' feel
of Death, no smell of its decay. Beneath a collapsed canopy, encrusted
all with gemstones, a shield of monsters. The treasure of a king
for sure; but not his body; King Anna's Cenotaph, the body lost
for ever in the flood plains of the Loidis. It is a strong, strong thing
a tomb without a corpse or hint of one. At whatever cost
volk will bring the body back unless it's scarred, devoid of hope
and bloated).

    "Dont speculate," said Ram, "leave singing to the Scop.

The Scop not you is there to guard the ancient Word Hoard of the Race.
Aneirin and Taliesin did it for the Welsh. Holder of the orb and sword
of State; the King. In contrast the Scop, the poet who can trace
the river mouth to the first icicle. An expansive Modern Word
Hoard's what we need."

    Upon the marble square *"Decorum est"*.
Jude says the phrase aloud. "No more, no less. The way we reach
up to the stars is through transmission, yet at the best
of memory there is a blank. For try as hard as each
one tries, we can't describe a lover's shining face
exactly as it is. We focus in. The nose, the eyes, the teeth
all are recalled but not as a totality. There's not the grace
and favour of full memory of she who lies beneath.

Karen: "Fame and Fortune are partners, that is sometimes said,
coupled together meshing and coo–coo–cooing in a nuptial bed."

Apart from the small neon sign which just says *Dodi*, and upon the
marble square a date, one–nine–nine–seven, there's little else but an
Artist's Installation in which an ancient sleeps beside three
tables.

    Jude:"What is that's antecedence?"

          Ram:"An old man
often sits upon a stacking chair beside a pasting table
at car boots. This is a themed place. Here things look
of something that's well known.

          A heavy duty cable
links to *Ikea* spot lights which enlighten the *Table Of The Book*.

The one that stands upon the sagging stall is not a Book of Life.
No Bible, Qur'an, Torah, the Guru Granth Sahib or Rig Vedas,
but the pop–up book which shows our Prince kissing his wife
upon the Bucking Balcony; Though almost perfect it is crass
is *Charles and Diana. The Wedding Book*.

          "What else is there to see?"

"Well, not a lot." Upon the final table stands a rather grand TV.

Unity of Theme.

      Dodi had watched The Royal Wedding on TV
and this is it, Al Fayed's set, *Exhibit Uno*. It rests upon a plastic stand
just by the door. A *Harrod's Hebronite With Gold Damask*. You see
the same at every *Dixons* though not its marble box.

          An ivory band,
runs around the top, it's Rhino horn. Jude can't recall
a nobler stand or television set than this. Encrusted
diamonds stapled to *Velcro* cover tuning dials. All in all
a silvered set with anchored hallmark.

        Those who've lusted
after status love such sets. It is the sort Sue–Ellen watched
in Dallas; gin bottle by her side, is like the one the poor, sad Shah
of Persia owned before that Shi'ite saint came back and snatched
the Peacock Throne, then sold that chair for guns.

        It is an who–la–la
made for the nouveau riche, *Dixons* into Knightsbridge, made to impress.

And yet on it Dodi saw a marriage peck of Prince and Welsh Princess.

The Wedding Video is still on. The little Arab man upon his folding
chair is still asleep: "He looks the simple sort who'll snatch
his forty winks and rise refreshed." says Jude. "He's holding
in his hand the channel changer, and on a thin, thin wrist a watch
that has a plastic strap. Its face, a rabbit's face. And at his feet
a mug of Charles and Di (*Ich Dien*). The coffee is clap cold.

My grandad had the look of him. His clothes were neat
and tidy like this man's, Jude meditates. "Why do we hold
a channel changer when we'd easily change the world
into a better place by action, yet if we take just forty winks
the Men of May will move and grapple; one hand curled
to clutch the throat, the other rooting in my purse." Jude thinks
about Old Father Thames. "In its oiled silt my silver coin.
Who'll trough for it not them; no more the Gadarene swine?"

"Excuse me sir, but who are you?"
                              The old man stirs in sleep
then one eye opens.
                 (In Castleford an Argos clock
goes off before the minute hand had reached Nirvana)
                                        "Weep
for all Mankind," he says, "for Mankind is on trial, is in the dock.
All is not going as it should. But since you're here and heaven sent,
you're just in time. In times of need you seem to know this place."

Jude comes straight out. "Are you the man who made Gadhafi's tent?
That is a wonder tent for sure. Peasants sit inside in grace
and favour while that Prince of Men, the Lion of the Libyans,
gives them dates, and lists of dates, to eat or scan. They look towards
the East for steady futures and for hints. Exactly what he plans
for them is still unsure, he's in delay yet knows a lot of words.
That wonder tent stands by the sea, close to the ruins of Carthage?
He nods.
         "You are," says Jude, "for all Ages, though in the Modern Age."

[134]

"I am a maker of designer tents but not an architect. I do not make
the roadways in the sky, the sort you see upon the Dockland's line as trains
move fast on from the Bank."
                              He then speaks to the boy.
                                            "Take
time to think," and then with emphasis, "when come to list your Gains
and Losses. Count up to ten before you speak and say
why is it noble men who make tents and social outcasts
who build flats as *route–ways in the sky*, always pause but display
great erudition. You have power to change things. Elastoplasts
are good on a grazed knee or a scuffed fist but something more
substantial is required if you'd design then build housing for
a people. More resources aren't enough, you need a core
which does not rest on common sense. Be sure
in your philosophy, when building do not compromise."
                                            "He's shrewd"
she thinks.
          He turns and stares. "Say what will you do Jude?"

Jude thinks: "It's powerful talk. I'll think about the way
we have lost out."
                  The Man: "Upon the day when all your vanities burn
there won't be time to think. When you're aflame you cannot stay
to talk about philosophy. Who'll be your sentinel? Who'll take their turn
beside your bonfire, who'll rake your ash. Dodi must here have a tomb
and Mandy has a restaurant, that's worth looking for, but who will bid
your friends to drink at your quiet Wake."
                                    Jude is alarmed:
                                            "I hope they comb
my hair and set a lily in my hand before they hammer on the oaken lid."

Here Ram butts in to ebb the flow.
                        "That's really what is wrong
with Dodi's cenotaph, it lacks clear narrative and there's no
dream time. No time to look around in leisure or sing old songs,
no space for sing–along and none for doodling, no sacred cow
to look upon in pastures new; all is austerity and yet there is a style
in which the overall effect is laughable."
                                    Jude does not smile

[135]

she just looks on: "The space is sepulchre white, the rites
Islamic but beneath the marble slab no bones, no crucifix
to hint Redemption, just lines of shoes. Not sights
you'd see inside a Christian Church. The sacred mix
that makes the Jesus tale compelling; the narrative
of peasants in a vine yard or fisherman who cast
nets to fish for souls while hearing the Beatitudes. 'Give
of the best there is but also think on Death. This lot won't last,'
is just not here. This is a place where one small mullah calls
you to your prayers. Perhaps that's why the night grows wild
with yearning. This is a mosque. There's calligraphy upon the walls
not images of saints, of lambs and gentle Jesus meek and mild,
just the world of God seen by Mohammed; Kufic carved in ebonite,
script to cleanse men of their sins."

> In graffiti: "What a man will write

in sand is spoiled by foot prints."

> "Now what exactly does that mean?"

she asks. The old man does not answer he just rises
from his chair and with, "I'm going for a walk, Ive seen
enough of life and now would go on Hadj," departs.

> Jude: "If life comprises

increments and accidents he's worth his weight in gold for sure,
for he has gravitas. He seemed to focus long on Karen's lad
but why I am not sure. Perhaps I come to understand. If there's a cure
for modern life, why then he'll know it for he has clearly had
experience by the cart load. Don't stand about, its cold."
she shouts.

> "Don't fuss I'm champion," comes echoing back.

"I've heard that line before in family history, in the deja vue of old, old
problems; sentiment for my own place, that's the crack
which breaks their mould. Even if I'll soon be dead
yet I'll be curious."

> "Listen," says Karen, "Someone's up ahead."

Jude listens to the echoing of retreating, well shod feet.
"That's odd they're Manolo Blahnik; upper class
shoes. Was the Mandy that I sought not *Our* Mandy? Retreat
into yourself'. She stares about. "That way my time will pass
until I meet the girl who is ahead. I'm not profound
but then the space between us both is great. Her type
and mine are different types. I'm always curious, sound
in life and limb. In contrast she's a girl of style and hype.

Upon the quay a cannon booms the hour. Jude thinks upon Redemption
"This is a simple cenotaph, an empty dome just like the edge of space,
a canopy of plastic resting on twelve tilting posts. Ascension
into heaven might be possible from here, but clearly my place
isn't in the South but in the North. In London I'm just a bag
woman who slobs about carrying sacks; a goth, a pitiful hag.

And yet I've ample dignity. The opportunities for change are vast.
We don't need Domes near London Town or need to spend
three Giros on a trip down south. To stand tip–toe upon the mast
on Emley Moor is quite enough — Castleford's real clear — and send
your heart westward's across the Pennines into Lancashire. Better go
to Gujurat or Bangladesh, slow boat to China, find what is true
at Varanasi or on the clipper ships that travel from Typhoo; show
yourself in Asia, stay the month, and that way recognise your added value.
Just don't come here.
               ·I've added value. Yet who'll record my life
when I have gone. I am not great or very good. I'm known
within my family as *Our Jude*, as Trouble and Strife,
but they are nicknames, really I am loved. I'm shown
compassion there, and yet I choose to move along, to roam."

She hums her grandad's song *There Is No Place Like Home.*

Her final speech.
        "There's *Unity of Place* and that's for sure. You need
to know yourself, that's all you need. Avoid the hype which
says the future can be seen in three tired hours down here. Don't read
the Sunday glossies for what's going off in Greenwich, but stitch
experience for it comes in increments. Think through exactly who
you are and why you're here. Learn to talk to anyone. Don't sneer
at people on the Royston Bus but question them. Be true
and know your place, this above all else. Your place is now, not here.

Unity of Time.
        It's taken just on half a day to find
this out but time is never wasted if you keep
a journal or write some epic verse. Analysis is all. Behind
a good idea there's always better ones. Do not "Weep
for Zion," just get out there, meet Action Girls and daring dos.
There's more to life than hype, and more than Blahnik shoes."

Dave: "Let us to bed. This poem's over long. It's Albert Square;
straight Grant and Tiffany. The twang is oft times cockney,
almost Pearly King and yet it is about the share
we all must have in progress. Learn, look and see;
if you're on fire you'll find your neighbours burn.
Destroy democracy and it's into the pit to get
what you deserve. Young mothers first, it's your turn
now. Into the box with Judy. It is for real. They aren't set
piece these focus groups. Watch it. Make way for Mr Punch.

Numbing and cheapening down at first seem virtues. Build
capital projects—beer and circuses for Greenwich, brunch
by Colonel K, tills by Shirley Porter. Ask what' been killed
by dumbing.
        So why not after me: *New Labour and No schism*.
Into the pit. Spin doctors have small room for symbolism".

Karen: "Oh wise sweet man, oh brave new world. You've hit
a chord, have touched my wonder button and the
light's come on."
　　　　　She sees all clearly. The manly bit
and bob she wants stands there before her. The key
is but a man who she knew; Zarathustra–Dave. And if
he once had wandered off to Ropergate to cash a Giro
so what, he has come back refreshed, renewed. The biff
bang, wallop of that past is melted snow. The common biro
signs the Switch Card not the fountain pen. The Common thing
and common sense here transforms all, they're all we need to get us
through the wormhole we call life.

　　　　　　　　　　　　From out his pocket comes a ring.
Dave gives it to her with "Do not mind a tinker's cuss
what the world thinks. See me as I am, a friend who now will state
the bloody obvious."
　　　　　　　They kiss. "I love you Karen Micklethwaite."

Zarathustra–Dave, the ex and she have come together. It's not
a tomb, this truly is a place of family values, all is neat
and tidy, but almost empty. That much, let's all agree. The rot
has not set in. *Happy Ever After* is well urged.
　　　　　　　　　　　　"You can knit snot
you see," a drollery jokes. "They've done it here, upon this spot
the mess that comes when romance meshes. Human terrors
here can be constrained! It's a matter of faith! You've got
to believe in Mills and Boon, in this *Comedy Of Errors*;
just take life *As You Like It*. Tea with three sugar sachets, weak?"

"We found that *Mandy's Place* was just a Greasy Spoon. The spin
was on promotion.
　　　　　　　Karen now. "Place any name inside *The Guardian*
and see the chattering classes flock. Mandy's caf remember bought in
something equal to the GNP of a modest Indian State or Bantustan.
But money's not enough.

　　　　　　　　"Let's drink their toast but not in wines."
Their best man's on his feet. The young son speaks his final lines

"I stand before all here today as the first born. I'll speak
few words so listen to this carefully. You're here to learn
and learn you will. Get this and get it straight. The weak
and poor, and those that weep a bucketful, are no concern
of mine. Into the pit with them.
                                    The Man Who'll Live
For Ever has been born, and born of Woman and of Man,
as was foretold. Science gently rocks as we contrive
to bind Prometheus. He's here and now. All goes to plan.

We've built to test destruction and can build a Master Race.
Let's do it now. Let's not equivocate but move the action on.
We all need bread and jobs not circuses. We need a living space
and can't afford to argue or to wait for it. The time for talkings gone.
Now we must act. Enough of blair, blair, blair and blah, blah, blah.
I've changed my name from Micklethwaite to Ali Akbar Shah."

The calendar started off in middle June, the year was six two two,
the place, Medina ten years before the Prophet (Peace Be On Him) died.
Few are Christian so why Millennium? In the Dome you do not get a clue
about the constraint or elegance of living simply. Anyone who's tried
to find a way around this ignorance has failed. When you sow
a modified grain you reap corruption. All's rotten in the State,
all's hype and bombast; ignorance. A minority know their elbow
from their arse, so can add up. This year is thirteen seventy eight"

At this the Dome begins to shake. He's lanced the festering boil,
and from the place they thought a tomb, but was a cenotaph, a stream
of yellow puss. At the boundaries smart pavilions collapse. Oil
on troubled water cannot stop this flow. Karen begins to scream:
"Have pity Lord."
                        Dave the Designer: "All's vicious for all's crude."

Pragmatic ever: "Let's get out of here" says honest Jude."

Epilogue

Please make my lines at least agreeable,
for though my verses often lack a syllable
because my effort is not seen
in graces, look to what I mean."

Geoffrey Chaucer. *The House of Fame*

In London Town most part are carrion the rest
are crows who pick at it, know this, know all.
The fit survive and some explore, for the test
of survival lies in guess work. Progress, call
it what you will, comes by chance in increments;
there never is a master plan. If the empty Dome
is Mandy's Restaurant or Dodi's Tomb, the tents
of the Philistine horde, the start of Kingdom Come
or the back of Bill's Mothers, rest assured
that there's a price to pay and the poor will just
go on and pay it. Spin doctors will ensure they're cured
of doubt; the medicine's called hype. Put your trust
in politicians if that takes your fancy, but it
is rarely good to tell the truth. Into the Pit.

"The present is a real gift that's why its called
the present." In the words we find in books
of sentimental–kitsch lies wisdom. Appalled
by insight scholars will back off. What looks
to be intellectual small fry can be the true
wisdom of the age. *Theres No Place Like Home*
still has a real resonance. Remember little is new
in life. Consider this. Fill the Millennium Dome
with all you find spread out upon a pasting table
at a car boot sale but blow them to their outer limit,
and you won't show old England at its best. What you are able
to do with synthetics is almost limitless but does each bit
and bob gain worth with expansion? Not really. Modern materials
have some status but do they make us focus on cathedrals?

THE END

Mandy's Place in the Expanded Field
By David Godber

There never was a master plan. Everyone almost drifted towards a very original approach to a most unusual Combined Arts project.

Brian Lewis was appointed Visiting Fellow in Verse and Fine Art at Loughborough University in 1998 in order to work with students and staff in projects which crossed boundaries between the visual, literary and performative aspects of creativity, as well as to draw sustenance from the environment provided by a thriving School of Art. Among other things that year he asked Colin Rhodes, who teaches Art History there, to write an introduction to his new anti–Art–Establishment poem, *The Bus to Hope*. When Rhodes also unexpectedly sent him a quirky drawing of the writer as a seated 'Sculptor in Bedlam', Lewis incorporated it into the final design. Previously Lewis had himself drawn a picture at the front of each of the Cantos of his poems in the tradition of Oskar Kokoschka, George Grosz and Michael Ayrton, but now he found himself working with someone who was adding a new dimension to the written text. Recognising that, it seemed natural to Lewis to ask Rhodes if he would work with him on a new Millennium piece which would become 1999's *Jude* poem.

The brief for Rhodes, as for the other artists who subsequently became involved in the Combined Arts project which took *Looking for Mandy's Place* as a starting point, was simple: read the poem and react visually to it. There was no comment or joint discussion with Lewis about the nature and meaning of the work; only after a piece was completed did they talk about it. At this stage either one of them might make adjustments to their work. They were anxious to develop a symbiotic working relationship, rather than one in which the work of the illustrator became subservient to the text.

There is no need here to discuss the evolution of the poem, though it might be useful to make two points. Lewis prefers to work with actors and is therefore used to a director asking for modifications to text either in the interest of greater clarity or to make dramatic impact. During the genesis of his long works, he also habitually solicits advice on the way that a narrative should run. Given its London setting, it is perhaps not surprising that the poem initially contained scant reference to Loughborough. However, because of Lewis' increasingly close association with the place, Mario Minichiello suggested during a *read–around–the–room* session at the University in December that it might be appropriate to include something about the town and the demise of its industry, and in particular the closure of Ladybird Books. As a result, Lewis wrote a new Canto featuring Loughborough and this part of the narrative became the focus of Andy Selby's visual contribution.

Earlier long poems in the *Jude* series followed a simple design pattern. The narrative was broken into Cantos, each with an illustration as a frontispiece. When Rhodes took over as illustrator he had this elementary job brief and the knowledge that in *Looking for Mandy's Place* there were likely to be nine Cantos plus a Prologue and Epilogue. When he got down to the finished drawings he did not proceed through the book in a logical manner, but 'emerged' from the text at points at which the strongly–felt images occurred to him. Thus, the drawing for Canto 6 was the first, Canto 1 the second, and so on.

Rhodes' normal practice is to work up an elaborate sketch and then deconstruct until he finds its essence. Instead in these drawings he found satisfaction with the preliminary phase of ballpoint pen drawing and worked up place–specific settings in which a cast of characters invented by Lewis were selected out and interpreted. Key figures, such as Jude, the children, Ram, Mandy and Zarathustra became incorporated in drawings. Others, such as Mills and Boon and the old Moslem man did not. In physique and dress all are very much his creatures because when writing Lewis will describe personality and history, but not the look of his people. This is because he knows that too specific a description makes problems in casting—say that Jude is small and overweight and you cannot use a thin actress. Rhodes, therefore, was able to devise his own 'cast' in response to the text. Thus, the original inspiration for Karen walking in Greenwich is a young woman in an old photograph of Doncaster, her daughter the artist's youngest child.

At first Rhodes shied away from depicting Jude at all. She seemed too precious, too much a part of someone else's mythology. But the need for her presence in the image of sunset described by Lewis in Canto 9 eventually became overwhelming. To make this work visually Jude had to be slim. Having done this, Rhodes then made a crucial decision; he made Jude black. There was no textual support for this. On the other hand, there was no reason why she should not be. When he saw the drawing it took Lewis by surprise, but rather than see it as something that ought to be discussed and resolved to their mutual satisfaction, he chose to accept the 'black girl' interpretation without reservation. By immediately taking it on board and seeing it as something that enhanced the poem, he showed that this was a collaborative venture and not one in which he was the sole proprietor. Lewis had seen Jude as a local girl from Castleford—a predominantly white area—but saw advantages in making his principle character extra–ordinary. Yet, the likeness of Jude owes more to Rhodes than it does to any ideas the writer held in his head but did not express on paper.

In a different way to Rhodes, the sculptor Dave Morris is here interested in certain place–specific architectural forms found near the banks of the Thames. The Millennium Dome, the Royal Observatory, Canary Wharf and the clipper *Cutty Sark* all find a place in his sculpture, as well as a series of large drawings inspired by the poem's sense of place. Characteristically, the sublime jostles with the ridiculous. Morris and printmaker and papermaker Karen Legg had different problems from the rest of the contributors because of the nature of their practice; having to distil a few ideas from Lewis' poem they reduced a long piece of writing to visual statements which move towards the abstract. Legg's paper pulp and pigment pieces are even more distanced from narrative reaction to the text, referring in a much more conceptual way to some of the overtly political themes. She narrows her focus down to food, a dominant subject in Canto Three. Having acquired some genetically modified cereals, she has reduced them to fibre and incorporated them into handmade paper. Placed beside a twin work made from natural fibres they seem identical, yet they are different in this important, invisible way.

By contrast, the painter Harry Malkin, illustrators Mario Minichiello, Andy Selby and Gary Taylor, and the graphic designer Mark Wood seem to have almost too much choice. All have commented on the oddness of this collaboration, for all are used to working to detailed briefs from commissioning editors and art directors who are rarely creatively involved in the textual element of a project. Lewis, as we have seen, avoids the set brief; he will explain text, but not proscribe any course of action. This has therefore been an attractive proposition. As Minichiello says, 'In commercial projects the agenda for what is produced has been rigidly set and is made explicit within the briefing documentation. As a result these are never truly collaborative. Lewis, however, has no other agenda beyond the production of the printed text.'

The Millennium celebration is supposed to be an outpouring of community spirit. Yet, there seems to be little evidence of this in officially sponsored preparations for the celebration. But why should there be? This is an artificial event. As often happens in the arts the more vital expressions of our heterogeneous cultural condition are found in oppositional works, and it is those who adopt a critical stance who best express the popular mood. In this instance opposition is articulated by combining the arts in an unusual way and when the collaborators do this they use social notions which go back to the aesthetics of Aristotle. In the Prologue Lewis declares his attachment to the Unities and delivers a story of a day or so, taking no longer than one revolution of the Earth. The Place is Greenwich and the theme artificiality, or, to focus through a modern word, 'hype'.